The Power of the European Court of Justice

The European Court of Justice (ECJ) has played a vital role in promoting the process of European integration. In recent years, however, the expansion of EU law has led it to impact ever more politically sensitive issues, and controversial ECJ judgments have elicited unprecedented levels of criticism. Can we expect the Court to sustain its role as a motor of deeper integration without Member States or other countervailing forces intervening? To answer this question, we need to revisit established explanations of the Court's power to see if they remain viable in the Court's contemporary environment. We also need to better understand the ultimate limits of the Court's power – the means through which and extent to which national governments, national courts, litigants and the Court's other interlocutors attempt to influence the Court and to limit the impact of its rulings.

In this book, leading scholars of European law and politics investigate how the ECJ has continued to support deeper integration and whether the EU is experiencing an increase in countervailing forces that may diminish the Court's ability or willingness to act as a motor of integration.

This book was published as a special issue of the *Journal of European Public Policy*.

Susanne K. Schmidt is Professor of Political Science at the University of Bremen.

R. Daniel Kelemen is Jean Monnet Chair and Professor of Political Science at Rutgers University.

Journal of European Public Policy Series
Series Editor: Jeremy Richardson is a Professor at Nuffield College, Oxford University

This series seeks to bring together some of the finest edited works on European Public Policy. Reprinting from Special Issues of the *Journal of European Public Policy*, the focus is on using a wide range of social sciences approaches, both qualitative and quantitative, to gain a comprehensive and definitive understanding of Public Policy in Europe.

Towards a Federal Europe
Edited by Alexander H. Trechsel

The Disparity of European Integration
Edited by Tanja A. Börzel

Cross-National Policy Convergence: Causes Concepts and Empirical Findings
Edited by Christoph Knill

Civilian or Military Power? European Foreign Policy in Perspective
Edited by Helene Sjursen

The European Union and New Trade Politics
Edited by John Peterson and Alasdair R. Young

Comparative Studies of Policy Agendas
Edited by Frank R. Baumgartner, Christoffer Green-Pedersen and Bryan D. Jones

The Constitutionalization of the European Union
Edited by Berthold Rittberger and Frank Schimmelfenig

Empirical and Theoretical Studies in EU Lobbying
Edited by David Coen

Mutual Recognition as a New Mode of Governance
Edited by Susanne K. Schmidt

France and the European Union
Edited by Emiliano Grossman

Immigration and Integration Policy in Europe
Edited by Tim Bale

Reforming the European Commission
Edited by Michael W. Bauer

International Influence Beyond Conditionality
Postcommunist Europe after EU enlargement
Edited by Rachel A. Epstein and Ulrich Sedelmeier

The Role of Political Parties in the European Union
Edited by Björn Lindberg, Anne Rasmussen and Andreas Warntjen

EU External Governance
Projecting EU Rules beyond Membership
Edited by Sandra Lavenex and Frank Schimmelfennig

EMU and Political Science
What Have We Learned?
Edited by Henrik Enderlein and Amy Verdun

Learning and Governance in the EU Policy Making Process
Edited by Anthony R. Zito

Political Representation and EU Governance
Edited by Peter Mair and Jacques Thomassen

Europe and the Management of Globalization
Edited by Wade Jacoby and Sophie Meunier

Negotiation Theory and the EU
The State of the Art
Edited by Andreas Dür, Gemma Mateo and Daniel C. Thomas

The Political Economy of Europe's Incomplete Single Market
Edited by David Howarth and Tal Sadeh

The European Union's Foreign Economic Policies
A Principal-Agent Perspective
Edited by Andreas Dür and Michael Elsig

The Politics of the Lisbon Agenda
Governance Architectures and Domestic Usages of Europe
Edited by Susana Borrás and Claudio M. Radaelli

Agency Governance in the European Union
Edited by Berthold Rittberger and Arndt Wonka

The EU Timescape
Edited by Klaus H. Goetz and Jan-Hinrik Meyer-Sahling

The EU's Common Foreign and Security Policy
Edited by Helene Sjursen

Economic Patriotism in Open Economies
Edited by Ben Clift and Cornelia Woll

The Power of the European Court of Justice
Edited by Susanne K. Schmidt and R. Daniel Kelemen

The Power of the European Court of Justice

Edited by
Susanne K. Schmidt and R. Daniel Kelemen

Routledge
Taylor & Francis Group
LONDON AND NEW YORK

First published 2013
by Routledge
4 Park Square, Milton Park, Abingdon, Oxon, OX14 4RN

Simultaneously published in the USA and Canada
by Routledge
605 Third Avenue, New York, NY 10017

Routledge is an imprint of the Taylor & Francis Group, an informa business

This book is a reproduction of the *Journal of European Public Policy*, vol. 19, issue 1. The Publisher requests to those authors who may be citing this book to state, also, the bibliographical details of the special issue on which the book was based.

British Library Cataloguing in Publication Data
A catalogue record for this book is available from the British Library

ISBN 13: 978-0-415-62788-7 (hbk)

Typeset in Times New Roman
by Taylor & Francis Books

Publisher's Note
The publisher would like to make readers aware that the chapters in this book may be referred to as articles as they are identical to the articles published in the special issue. The publisher accepts responsibility for any inconsistencies that may have arisen in the course of preparing this volume for print.

Contents

Citation Information

The chapters in this book were originally published in the *Journal of European Public Policy*, volume 19, issue 1 (January 2012). When citing this material, please use the original page numbering for each article, as follows:

Chapter 1
Introduction – the European Court of Justice and legal integration: perpetual momentum?
R. Daniel Kelemen and Susanne K. Schmidt
Journal of European Public Policy, volume 19, issue 1 (January 2012)
pp. 1-7

Chapter 2
Who cares about nationality? The path-dependent case law of the ECJ from goods to citizens
Susanne K. Schmidt
Journal of European Public Policy, volume 19, issue 1 (January 2012)
pp. 8-24

Chapter 3
The reference points of EU judicial politics
Damian Chalmers and Mariana Chaves
Journal of European Public Policy, volume 19, issue 1 (January 2012)
pp. 25-42

Chapter 4
The political foundations of judicial independence in the European Union
R. Daniel Kelemen
Journal of European Public Policy, volume 19, issue 1 (January 2012)
pp. 43-58

Chapter 5
Do ECJ judges all speak with the same voice? Evidence of divergent preferences from the judgments of chambers

Michael Malecki
Journal of European Public Policy, volume 19, issue 1 (January 2012)
pp. 59-75

Chapter 6
Activism relocated. The self-restraint of the European Court of Justice in its national context
Gareth Davies
Journal of European Public Policy, volume 19, issue 1 (January 2012)
pp. 76-91

Chapter 7
Rights adjudication and constitutional pluralism in Germany and Europe
Alec Stone Sweet and Kathleen Stranz
Journal of European Public Policy, volume 19, issue 1 (January 2012)
pp. 92-108

Chapter 8
With Luxembourg in mind ... the remaking of national policies in the face of ECJ jurisprudence
Michael Blauberger
Journal of European Public Policy, volume 19, issue 1 (January 2012)
pp. 109-126

Chapter 9
Perpetual momentum: directed and unconstrained?
Fritz W. Scharpf
Journal of European Public Policy, volume 19, issue 1 (January 2012)
pp. 127-139

Introduction – the European Court of Justice and legal integration: perpetual momentum?

R. Daniel Kelemen and Susanne K. Schmidt

The European Court of Justice (ECJ)[1] has played an indispensible role as a motor of European integration. In judgments addressing the balance between national and supranational authority, the European Court – not unlike high courts in other federal-type systems (Bzdera 1993; Halberstam 2008; Volcansek 2008) – has demonstrated a bias in favour of centralization. Again and again, the ECJ has demonstrated the independence and the authority necessary to push the scope and depth of European integration beyond what European Union (EU) law-makers had intended. The literature on the European legal integration establishes a number of reasons for this marked bias towards supranationality: there is a comparatively weak legislator at the supranational level and divisions between EU law-makers generate gridlock and open up space for the ECJ to pursue its pro-integration preferences (Pollack 2003; Stone Sweet 2004: 7–9; Tallberg 2002); European lawyers worked early to establish the supremacy and direct effect of European law (Vauchez 2008); national lower courts have had incentives to refer cases to the ECJ through the preliminary ruling system (Alter 2001); private parties had incentives to make legal claims based on their economic rights and other individual rights under European law (Cichowski 2007; Conant 2002; Kelemen 2011). Together these factors have sparked a self-reinforcing process of judicialization that has expanded ECJ power and deepened integration (Stone Sweet 2004; Stone Sweet and Brunell 1998).

Some observers fear that in privileging integration over the safeguarding of national competences, the Court's jurisprudence may threaten the maintenance of a politically acceptable balance between European-level and national competences in the EU. Political controversy surrounding the ECJ's major integrative decisions is, of course, nothing new. Powerful national leaders from French President Giscard d'Estaing in the 1980s to German Chancellor Kohl in the 1990s have publicly attacked the court for its activism and overreach. In recent years, however, the expansion of EU law has led it to impact ever more politically sensitive issues. And today EU law treads on this sensitive terrain in a period when the 'permissive consensus' concerning European integration has faded. ECJ rulings in controversial cases such as the '*Laval* quartet' (i.e., *Laval*, *Viking*, *Luxembourg* and *Rüffert*) (see Malmberg 2010) and *Mangold* have elicited what many see as an unprecedented level of political criticism. This furore raises the question of whether the ECJ can maintain a politically acceptable balance of European and national competences, and the question of which political and legal factors influence its jurisprudence on this balance.

To date, the expansive jurisprudence of the ECJ seems unbroken. But in a more politically sensitive environment and in a Union that has grown to encompass 27 member states based on very different traditions of the rule of law, one might expect as much change as continuity.

This collection of contributions investigates how the ECJ has sustained its bias toward deeper integration and whether the EU is experiencing an increase in countervailing forces that may diminish the Court's ability or willingness to act as a motor of integration. Can we expect the dynamics of the Court's case law to continue as before without member states or other countervailing forces intervening? Other than national governments working to safeguard their authority, national courts and national bars might be expected to react negatively to continued ECJ expansionism where it threatens their authority.

To understand whether the Court can sustain its role as a motor of deeper integration, we need to revisit established explanations of the Court's power to see if they remain viable in the Court's contemporary environment. We also need to better understand the ultimate limits of the Court's power – the means through which and the extent to which national governments, national courts, litigants and the Court's other interlocutors attempt to influence the Court and to limit the impact of its rulings.

There are many glaring lacunae in our knowledge about European legal integration. Though the literature on legal mobilization in the EU has grown in recent years (for instance, Cichowski 2007; Kelemen 2011; Stone Sweet 2010), we still know far too little about the decision-makers at the heart of the EU's legal system – the justices of the ECJ. Unlike the United States Supreme Court, the ECJ publishes no votes or dissenting opinions, making it difficult to conduct analyses assessing the impact of the justices' policy preferences. Based on the ECJ's pro-integration track record, many assume that ECJ judges always favour integration over the safeguarding of national competences. But can this assumption hold, given that the judges are, after all, appointed by their member state government, having been socialized in their national legal system? Likewise, we still know far too little about the conditions under which private litigants actually claim their European rights in front of national courts. How does the interaction between the ECJ and these courts take place? Given these institutional conditions, how can we explain the way that case law develops? Finally, we know too little about the impact of the ECJ's case law on member states. Though there is a growing literature on 'Europeanization' of public policy, there is still no equivalent in studies of European law to the extensive literature on 'impact analysis' conducted by scholars of American public law (but see Conant [2002] for a notable exception). Europeanization studies have predominantly been concerned with the transposition and implementation of European secondary law – directives and regulations (Börzel 2001), and have largely neglected the reactions to case law (Töller 2010).

We should also note what we cannot do. With the broad focus on revisiting and refining our established explanations of the ECJ's power, we do not purport to take exhaustive account of major ongoing changes that arguably would merit a special collection in their own right. The accession of 12 new member states with very different legal traditions is a major change, and not much is known yet of its implications for the EU's judicial system, particularly if we include the relationship with the lower and constitutional courts in the new member states. We therefore restrict the discussion of enlargement to its impact on the aggregate level in so far as it is already apparent there, for instance in terms of the increase of judges, or conflict lines (*Laval*). Other developments to be noted are the increasing impact of the case law of the ECJ on national criminal law, and the changes brought about by the Charter of Fundamental Rights, and the accession to the European Convention on Human Rights.

This collection assembles a number of renowned scholars and more junior scholars conducting cutting edge research on the ECJ. It brings together both political scientists and lawyers and explores legal integration from the perspectives of both disciplines. Collectively, the contributions explore a number of central themes.

How do the composition and structure of the ECJ influence its jurisprudence? Might the appointment by some governments of more Eurosceptic judges influence the Court's jurisprudence? Malecki's (2012) innovative research suggests that some judges may indeed hold more Eurosceptic preferences and that the presence of more Eurosceptic judges on chambers of the court is associated with those chambers making decisions that are less supportive of European integration. More generally, in recent years as it has expanded to 27 judges, the Court has dramatically reorganized the way it conducts its work, hearing more and more cases in 'chambers' composed of subsets of judges. While decisions are taken in the name of the ECJ as a whole, in fact most decisions are made by groups of three or five judges. Does reliance on a chamber system pose a risk to the coherence of ECJ jurisprudence, or has the system been structured in a way that is likely to maintain the coherence of the law and safeguard the independence of the Court (Kelemen 2012)?

How sensitive is the court to political attacks? As mentioned above, the Court has been subject to an unprecedented degree of political criticism in recent years (Blauberger 2012). But just how sensitive should we expect the Court to be to such criticism? Often, when governments increase political pressure on courts, this simultaneously increases normative pressure on courts to act in a 'countermajoritarian' fashion and to defend minority interests (Chalmers and Chaves 2012). Moreover, if the Court enjoys a high degree of diffuse public support relative to the politicians who criticize it, this may shield the Court against such criticisms (Kelemen 2012).

How do litigants, national courts and other members of the 'legal fields' involved in ECJ litigation influence the impact and course of ECJ jurisprudence? Though the ECJ is often portrayed as existing in a kind of 'splendid isolation' in Luxembourg, the Court is actually surrounded by specialized and often very circumscribed legal communities. These communities can empower the ECJ – by bringing cases to its docket, helping it to build up lines of case law in a path-dependent fashion (Schmidt 2012) and spreading its jurisprudence within national legal orders – but the very fact that these constituencies are limited in number, in specialization and in their interests may itself constrain the ECJ's impact (Chalmers and Chaves 2012).

How do national governments and national courts further react to or adapt to ECJ jurisprudence? The contributions go beyond simplistic dichotomies between compliance and non-compliance to explore the variety of ways in which national courts and national governments respond to ECJ decisions. The authors find that some national courts may rely on ECJ rulings in their conflicts with other courts within their national legal order (Stone Sweet and Stranz 2012) or that national courts may in fact build on ECJ rulings, offering more 'activist' interpretations than the ECJ had required (Davies 2012). National governments, for their part, may craft nuanced legislative strategies to mitigate the impact of controversial ECJ decisions, and the content of these strategies will vary depending on the political composition of the government in question (Blauberger 2012).

Where do the contributions in this collections leave us? First of all, very clearly, they show once again how characterizations of European integration along the supranationalist–intergovernmentalist divide miss the point (Schmidt 1996). Integration advances because the multilevel system offers an opportunity structure for (integrationist) changes not only to supranational but also to national private and public actors. Mobile litigants use European law to circumvent domestic legal constraints. National courts use the opportunity to strengthen their role in the national legal hierarchy, with single judges more often than not realizing specific legal – or policy – preferences in this way. As for the ECJ, the lack of institutionalized court-curbing mechanisms and an apparently functioning permissive consensus insulates it effectively from political pressure. While there are clear differences as to the preferences of the involved judges, the likelihood that member states can use their appointment power to alter the Court's interpretation towards a more autonomy-regarding course for the member states seem slight. The development of case law can be conceptualized as being path dependent – the entitlement to individual rights established with direct effect and the prohibition of a restriction of economic rights grounded in *Dassonville* and *Cassis* offers sufficient incentives to litigants to pursue an extension of the reach of European law.

Yet, the image of an expansionist ECJ does not stand undisputed in this collection. Only some areas of law advance to this extent, as Chalmers and Chaves (2012) argue, resulting in a very uneven development across legal fields. And according to Davies (2012), where this expansion does take place, it is not driven solely or even primarily by the ECJ, but rather is rooted in broad interpretations of EU law made by national courts. Finally, Michael Blauberger (2012) shows that even highly controversial judgments are absorbed in the domestic political process in a way that a new consensus becomes possible, eventually diminishing the impact of the ruling.

It remains to be seen whether (and, if so, when) the European Union may enter into a phase of consolidation as other federal-type systems have experienced (Bzdera 1993) – a phase in which the ECJ would act less as an engine of integration and more as balancer of EU ('federal-level') and national interests. It is clear, however, that the EU has not yet entered such a phase. And as Fritz Scharpf (2012) emphasizes in his conclusion to this collection, the dominant role of the ECJ results in a skewed constitutional balance. While authors disagree as to the extent of the ECJ's activism, the pro-integrative role of the European court system as a whole – including member states' courts and the ECJ – is undisputed.

Biographical notes: R. Daniel Kelemen is the Jean Monnet Chair, Director of the Center for European Studies and Associate Professor of Political Science at Rutgers University. Susanne K. Schmidt is Professor of Political Science and Dean of the Bremen International Graduate School of Social Sciences at the University of Bremen.

ACKNOWLEDGMENTS

Susanne Schmidt would like to acknowledge generous funding of the German Research Foundation via the CRC 597. We are very grateful to those colleagues who agreed to act as anonymous reviewers for the contributions. We would also like to thank those participants of the November 2010 workshop in Bremen that acted as discussants of the different papers: Philipp Genschel; Fritz Scharpf; Martin Höpner; Christian Joerges; Michael Blauberger; and Arndt Wonka. Daniel Kosak did a great job preparing the manuscript for this edited collection. Our special thanks go to Fritz Scharpf for agreeing to take over the conclusion!

NOTE

1 The Treaty of Lisbon introduced changes in the names of EU judicial institutions. The Court of Justice of the European Communities is now officially known as the 'Court of Justice' – but informally we can still refer to it as the European Court

of Justice or ECJ. The Court of First Instance is now known as the General Court. The EU's judiciary as a whole – including the ECJ, the General Court and the Civil Service Tribunal, and any lower courts that may be established in the future – are collectively referred to as the Court of Justice of the European Union (or CJEU).

REFERENCES

Alter, K.J. (2001) *Establishing the Supremacy of European Law – The Making of an International Rule of Law in Europe*, Oxford: Oxford University Press.

Blauberger, M. (2012) 'With Luxembourg in mind . . . the remaking of national policies in the face of ECJ jurisprudence', *Journal of European Public Policy* 19(1): 109–26.

Börzel, T.A. (2001) 'Non-compliance in the European Union: pathology or statistical artefact?', *Journal of European Public Policy* 8(5): 803–24.

Bzdera, A. (1993) 'Comparative analysis of federal high courts: a political theory of judicial review', *Canadian Journal of Political Science* 26(1): 3–29.

Chalmers, D. and Chaves, M. (2012) 'The reference points of EU judicial politics', *Journal of European Public Policy* 19(1): 25–42.

Cichowski, R. (2007) *The European Court, Civil Society, and European Integration*, Cambridge: Cambridge University Press.

Conant, L. (2002) *Justice Contained. Law and Politics in the European Union*, Ithaca, NY and London: Cornell University Press.

Davies, G. (2012) 'Activism relocated: the self-restraint of the European Court of Justice in its national context', *Journal of European Public Policy* 19(1): 76–91.

Halberstam, D. (2008) 'Comparative federalism and the role of the judiciary', in K.E. Whittington, R.D. Kelemen and G.A. Caldeira (eds), *The Oxford Handbook of Law and Politics*, Oxford: Oxford University Press, pp. 142–65.

Kelemen, R.D. (2011) *Eurolegalism: The Transformation of Law and Regulation in the European Union*, Cambridge, MA: Harvard University Press.

Kelemen, R.D. (2012) 'The political foundations of judicial independence in the European Union', *Journal of European Public Policy* 19(1): 43–58.

Malecki, M. (2012) 'Do ECJ judges all speak with the same voice? Evidence of divergent preferences from the judgments of chambers', *Journal of European Public Policy* 19(1): 59–75.

Malmberg, J. (2010) 'Posting post-Laval. international and national responses', *Working Paper No 5*, Uppsala: Uppsala Center for Labor Studies.

Pollack, M. (2003) *The Engines of Integration*, Oxford: Oxford University Press.

Scharpf, F.W. (2012) 'Perpetual momentum: directed and unconstrained?', *Journal of European Public Policy* 19(1): 127–39.

Schmidt, S.K. (1996) 'Sterile debates and dubious generalisations: European integration theory tested by telecommunications and electricity', *Journal of Public Policy* 16(3): 233–71.

Schmidt, S.K. (2012) 'Who cares about nationality? The path-dependent case law of the ECJ from goods to citizens', *Journal of European Public Policy* 19(1): 8–24.

Stone Sweet, A. (2004) *The Judicial Construction of Europe*, Oxford: Oxford University Press.

Stone Sweet, A. (2010) 'The European Court of Justice and the judicialization of EU governance', *Living Reviews in European Governance*, available at http://europeangovernance.livingreviews.org (accessed 23 December 2010).

Stone Sweet, A. and Brunell, T. (1998) 'Constructing a supranational constitution', *American Political Science Review* 92(1): 63–81.

Stone Sweet, A. and Stranz, K. (2012) 'Rights adjudication and constitutional pluralism in Germany and Europe', *Journal of European Public Policy* 19(1): 92–108.

Tallberg, J. (2002) 'Delegation to supranational institutions: why, how and with what consequences', *West European Politics* 25(1): 23–46.
Töller, A.E. (2010) 'Measuring and comparing the Europeanization of national legislation: a research note', *Journal of Common Market Studies* 48(2): 417–44.
Vauchez, A. (2008) 'The force of a weak field: law and lawyers in the government of the European Union (for a renewed research agenda)', *International Political Sociology* 2(2): 128–44.
Volcansek, M.L. (2008) 'Judicially crafted federalism: EU and USA', *EUSA Review* 21(1): 23–31.

Who cares about nationality? The path-dependent case law of the ECJ from goods to citizens

Susanne K. Schmidt

ABSTRACT The role that the ECJ plays in European integration has been much discussed by political scientists. Less is known about how case law develops. In this contribution, I give a historical–institutionalist account and argue that path dependence explains the course that case law takes. Litigants provide positive feedback in this process, aiming to strengthen their rights by transferring legal arguments from one area to the next, leading to a convergent interpretation of the fundamental freedoms. The contribution traces this development, analysing how legal arguments were transferred from goods markets to the free movement of workers and citizenship as a result of positive feedback to a distinct legal interpretation. I discard alternative explanations that explain case law by drawing on the preferences of member states or judges.

INTRODUCTION

In the literature, it is well recognized that the European Court of Justice (ECJ) managed to become an important actor for European integration (Stone Sweet 2010). By establishing the direct effect and supremacy of European law in the early 1960s, the ECJ constitutionalized the Treaty, granting European rights to individuals. The preliminary ruling procedure at the same time offered an institutional venue for individuals to enforce these new rights. Member states had to observe this process relatively helplessly. They may join court proceedings with observations (Granger 2004), but given the heterogeneity of preferences among them and the need to find unanimous positions to alter the Treaty and its legal interpretation, the Court is well shielded from member-state intervention. At the same time, the frustrations of an activist court are counterbalanced by the general interest and dependence on having a functioning independent umpire of controlling the implementation of agreements (Alter 2001).

While the strength of the ECJ is well established, the literature is not as advanced in explaining the course that the development of case law takes. Existing research provides several indications for explanations. The extreme positions here would be that judges either simply realize their own policy positions (Gely and Spiller 2008), or that they follow the preferences of the most powerful member states (Garrett 1995). Both interpretations face the problem that the precise content of the law does not matter: it is merely an empty shell that is either filled with the preferences of judges or those of their masters (Dyevre 2010). Against these alternative explanations, I argue that we can detect a path dependence of case law. More specifically, I argue that the interpretation of the freedom of movement of goods, as the area where the economy transnationalized first, served as a path for the interpretation of the other fundamental freedoms, supported by the positive feedback of private litigants. Had the case law originally been developed for another freedom, for instance services, another path of legal interpretation would have been likely. Positive feedback in this argument is caused by the litigious behaviour of private actors and the European Commission that take up existing arguments from the case law and transfer it to other fundamental freedoms. The Court, at the same time, is free to make reversals of its case law, and in fact this is something we repeatedly see in different areas. However, its overarching interest in the consistency of case law, often backed by litigants' support for the existing path, imply that the ECJ generally follows precedent. Compared to the alternative explanations of attributing case law to member states' or judges' preferences, this interpretation has the advantage of 'taking the law seriously' (Joerges 1996).

In this contribution, I will start by discussing this argument of a path dependence of case law, based on the legal interpretation for the free movement of goods, against alternative explanations. The argument of a path dependence is then 'tested' against developments in freedom of movement of workers and Union citizenship. Both cases can be seen as least likely because legally there would be good reasons for following a different legal interpretation.

THE DEVELOPMENT OF ECJ CASE LAW AS A PATH-DEPENDENT PROCESS

In the following, I will first present the concept of path dependence and apply it to case law. With its interpretation of the free movement of goods, I argue, the ECJ established a path that was then transferred to the other fundamental freedoms in a process of positive feedback. I close by discussing alternative explanations drawing on member states' and judges' preferences.

The concept of path dependence

Path-dependent processes were originally studied in the context of technical innovations, with the QWERTY keyboard being a very prominent example (David 1985). Later the idea was transferred to welfare states' institutional development (Pierson 2000). Characteristic of such processes is that the beginning of a path is contingent. The sequence of events and positive feedback, such as economies of scale or technical complementarities, result in a 'lock-in', making it highly unlikely to change a path once taken, even if it is inefficient (Mahoney 2000).

More recently, the concept has also been applied to case law, particularly focussing on the role of precedent (e.g., Fon *et al.* 2005). Reasoning by analogy allows courts to further legal certainty. They avoid appearing to be acting arbitrarily (i.e., politically) (Gerhardt 2005: 909). Only if similar cases are ruled in a similar manner can justice ever be established. Thus, precedent limits the range of permissible legal arguments, encouraging litigants to pursue certain legal claims rather than others.

By itself precedent is insufficient to argue for path dependence. On the one hand, stable equilibria in an area of law can result that lack the dynamism of a path-dependent process, fuelled by positive feedback.[1] On the other hand, frequent deviations from established case law show that precedent does not prohibit courts from pursuing alternative lines of reasoning. 'It is difficult to defend the assertion that precedents impose binding rules on judges, compelling them to decide individual cases in certain ways' (McCown 2003: 979). While the coherence of case law and legal certainty support precedent, there are also arguments favouring deviations, for instance that cases are not alike. I therefore follow Stone Sweet in his argument that it is precedent *together* with its motivating or de-motivating impact on litigants that establishes a path-dependent process.

> Legal institutions are path dependent to the extent that how litigation and judicial rule-making proceeds, in any given area of the law at any given point in time, is fundamentally conditioned by how earlier legal disputes in that area of the law have been sequenced and resolved. (Stone Sweet 2002: 113)

I will now turn to the question of the degree to which the ECJ's case law regarding the fundamental freedoms developed in a path-dependent way.

Path dependence in case law

As in other free trade areas, the provisions for the free movement of goods, services, workers and establishment[2] were formulated and originally interpreted as prohibitions of discrimination. Member states could not discriminate against those seeking economic activity in their markets, as long as they adhered to their domestic market regulations. In the famous cases of *Dassonville* (8/74) and *Cassis de Dijon* (120/78) in the 1970s, the ECJ changed this interpretation of the free movement of goods by arguing that national regulatory obligations could be treated as quantitative restrictions to trade. Member states have to take into account that market participants have already adhered to regulations in their home countries; these have to be mutually recognized. Additional regulatory burdens may only be required when being proportionate and justified by overriding public interests, as they pose 'a double burden' for market participants already regulated in their home country. The ECJ rarely grants member states this possibility (Oliver and Roth 2004). With the new argumentation based on a prohibition of restriction, implicitly member states traded enhanced market access for a loss of their regulatory autonomy (McCall Smith 2000). In a Community of nine member states with similar levels of economic development, they could assume equivalent market regulations.

Given the early internationalization of the goods trade, the new interpretation was originally established in this area. Stone Sweet and Brunell (2008: 9) provide data on the distribution of preliminary references across legal domains for the period 1958 to 2005. Litigation on goods has been important from the beginning, with 20.4 per cent of cases between 1958 and 1975, retaining its relative importance with 17.2 per cent in the period 2001–05. Similarly, for free movement of workers – albeit on a much lower level – we do not see significant changes with 3.2 per cent and 4.3 per cent respectively. Cases for establishment, in contrast, steadily grew from 2.4 per cent in 1958–75 up to 20.9 per cent in 2001–05. A similar development could probably be shown for services but they are not included in this data set.

The interpretation of the fundamental freedoms other than goods, that only slowly grew in importance over the years, such as establishment, stayed with the prohibition of discrimination for a longer time. However, the alternative interpretation as prohibition of restriction, which the ECJ pioneered in goods, offers private actors significant leeway. They can target all member state markets on the basis of their home regulation, and, moreover pick the member state with the lowest regulatory requirements for their establishment (Sun and Pelkmans 1995). Legally, interpreting the fundamental freedoms as a prohibition of restriction is a very different 'path' to the obligation of non-discrimination. The much greater leeway to pursue economic activities that such an interpretation offers is a significant incentive for litigants for extending this interpretation from the area of trade in goods to cover the other fundamental freedoms as well. Via their domestic courts and the preliminary ruling procedure, private actors have indirect access to the ECJ, allowing them to bring litigation that generates positive feedback, encouraging the case law to move down a path that extends their preferred interpretation to other fundamental freedoms.

An example is *Säger* (C-76/90), one of the first judgments transferring the reasoning of *Cassis* to services. Here, a patent-renewal alert service, established in the UK, had offered its services in Germany. This industry was more heavily regulated in Germany and a special licence was required which the company did not hold. The citation shows how the ECJ argued fully in parallel to the free movement of goods:

> Article 59 of the Treaty requires not only the elimination of all discrimination against a person providing services on the grounds of his nationality, but also the abolition of any restriction, even if it applies without distinction to national providers of services and to those of other Member States, when it is liable to prohibit or otherwise impede the activities of a provider of services

established in another Member State where he lawfully provides similar services (Summary, No. 1).

By granting additional rights, the ECJ motivates other actors to similarly use European Union (EU) litigation to their favour. To this important source of positive feedback I will turn now.

Sources of positive feedback

Which factors support the path dependence of case law and where does it find its limits? As mentioned, precedent furthers legal certainty, and it guards judges against appearing to rule politically. Particularly in a legally hierarchical setting such as in the EU, the ECJ depends on the co-operation of the courts in the member states in order to be effective. Lower courts will only be able to apply European law independently if the case law is consistent. This is also one incentive of the US Supreme Court to honour *stare decisis* (Bartels 2009: 475). However, courts, in particular courts of last instance, are not bound by precedent at all times. The cases reaching the ECJ or other constitutional or supreme courts are those where precedent does not give a clear hint towards the expected outcome. Otherwise the cases would not need to be treated at this level (Gerhardt 2005). Also, landmark judgments initiating new interpretations are not that rare. A well-known example is the *Keck* (C-267/91 and C-268/91) ruling, where the ECJ exempted selling arrangements from the reach of the free movement of goods. This was a response to an increase of cases on purely internal matters like shop opening hours (Rawlings 1993). It shows that judges are relatively free to break existing paths, or to start new legal traditions.

The path-dependence argument, in short, builds on the importance of precedent for courts but cannot be restricted to it. Feedback by private litigants is necessary. Not all possible paths are equally likely to get this support: litigants only follow up on case law that is beneficial to them. For instance, tax litigation before the ECJ typically reduces national revenue as litigants only pursue cases reducing their tax bills (Genschel and Jachtenfuchs 2011). A judgment like *Keck* that diminishes the scope of the freedoms, is therefore unlikely to spark litigant behaviour. No dynamic case law development takes place when positive feedback is lacking. Not all legal entitlements generate positive feedback: The fundamental freedoms grant individual rights to actors, furthering liberal notions of the public good, but hampering republican traditions that emphasize solidaristic against individual rights (Menéndez 2009: 27; Scharpf 2009).

The support of litigants provides legitimacy to the Court (and also to the Commission, for that matter) by showing that there is a positive response to the individual rights it has itself created. Similarly there is a widespread belief in the legal profession that member states have fallen short of delivering to citizens the 'promise' of European integration, and that the development of citizenship rights by the Court can bolster support for European integration (Aziz 2009: 282).

From the point of view of the ECJ, interpreting the different freedoms along similar lines strengthens the coherence of case law, given that often more than one freedom is relevant to a case. Figure 1 shows for infringement cases and preliminary references reaching the ECJ between 1990 and 2008 whether only a single or at least two freedoms were invoked for goods, services and the free movement of workers. While most goods cases concern exclusively this freedom, this is different for other freedoms, most notably for services, where, typically, several freedoms are cited as relevant. Consequently, once the logic of a prohibition of restrictions is transferred from goods to the other freedoms, there is much more pressure of pursuing a parallel approach to all freedoms in order to maintain the coherence of case law.

Path-dependent processes are difficult to interrupt, even if they lead to inefficient outcomes. The increased liberalization going along with an expansive interpretation of the fundamental freedoms is seen by some to increase efficiency; an economic argument that cannot be decided here. In this context, inefficiency refers to the political implications of the process. These concern, first of all, the judicialization of the policy process that takes decisions from the legislature to the courts. Secondly, redistributive implications arise from court decisions. Being less of a problem in the original area of goods, for services a reverse discrimination of nationals can result when service providers are subject to less stringent regulations (Schmidt 2009). Similarly, the freedom of establishment may allow the circumvention of tax and company law restrictions.

What are the scope conditions of such a path-dependent process to take off? Positive feedback through litigant behaviour requires that lower courts support the legal development by directing preliminary procedures to the ECJ. Also the lock-in of this path-dependent process can only result if a weak EU legislative

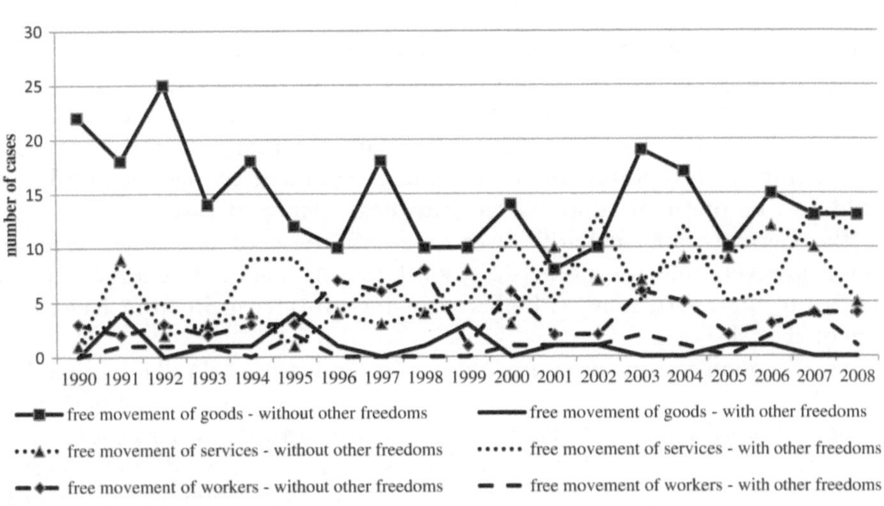

Figure 1 Two or more freedoms in one case
Source: EUR-LEX; personal calculations.

cannot redress problematic developments owing to demanding decision rules (Scharpf 2009).

Alternative explanations

Making a path-dependence argument has the advantage of according an independent influence to legal doctrine. Neither can be said of the two major contending schools of thought analysing judicial politics from a political science perspective, the attitudinal and the structural approach. Both approaches largely ignore legal doctrine – either judges follow their own policy preferences or those of the member states. However, if the content of legal texts does not contribute to Courts' decision-making, it becomes difficult to understand why rational actors would try to influence their final shape in the first place – or why it should make a difference whether courts can be overruled legislatively (Dyevre 2010: 311).

Nevertheless, these two explanations need consideration. The argument that the ECJ would merely follow the preferences of the larger member states was introduced into the 1990s debate on the ECJ by Garrett (1995). Later, Garrett and collaborators refined it, acknowledging that the ECJ would rule against the preferences of powerful member states whenever legal norms calling for such a ruling were well-established (Garrett *et al.* 1998). This argument needs no further discussion here, as the following analysis of the case law on workers and citizenship rights give ample examples where the court rules against the member states.

The question of judges' preferences is more difficult to refute. Since deliberations are confidential, and there are no dissenting opinions at the ECJ, we lack the empirical basis to analyse preferences. Based on a thought experiment, Kelemen (2012) finds that member states have little incentive to send judges with extreme – non-integrationist – preferences to the court. Decision-making by majority in the chambers would isolate them. Additional reasons speak against judges with extreme preferences. Judges can increase their impact with length of service, and a judge with medium preferences stands a better chance of reappointment should the government change. Such a judge would also be one that supports the path dependence of case law. Practices, like the German one, to hardly ever renew the term of the judge, seem to imply, however, that the domestic pay-off to patronage, of sending a party member to the court, may be higher than the expected gain from having an influential ECJ judge.

There are good reasons to assume that policy preferences of judges matter less rather than more at the EU than at the national level, given the rules of allocating cases to *rapporteurs* and to chambers. We can assume that the *rapporteur* to a case is most influential for its solution. Judges are never allocated cases concerning their home country. Moreover, there is no specialization among chambers as to case assignment. An arbitrary case allocation, however, makes it unlikely that judges can develop a specific line of argumentation across a series of cases.

Moreover, incentives to pursue specific policy preferences should be lower with no connection to the affected polity. Altogether it is likely that policy preferences play less of a role at the EU compared to the national level. The pay-off to building the EU's legal doctrine may be larger.

With no possibility of assessing judges' preferences empirically (but see Malecki [2012]), I therefore assume that the ECJ largely fosters its corporate self-interest of stabilizing and extending its own position. In as far as judges pursue, beyond that, individual preferences, these are more likely to be professional legal preferences than policy preferences.

To summarize: neither member states' nor judges' preferences can explain the development of case law as well as a historical-institutionalist explanation. Through a path-dependent process, fuelled by the positive feedback of litigant behaviour, I argue that the logic of a prohibition of restrictions was transferred from the free movement of goods to the other freedoms. While for the free movement of goods the *Cassis*-logic does not imply significant redistributive consequences, this is different for the other freedoms (Schmidt 2009). It is highly unlikely that a similarly far-reaching interpretation could have been established had it not been for the 'coincidence' of goods markets internationalizing first. Given the distributional issues being raised by this path, it can be regarded as inefficient in a political sense. To what extent, however, can we speak of a path leading to convergence also when regarding the freedom of workers and the rights of European citizenship?

THE FREE MOVEMENT OF WORKERS AND CITIZENSHIP RIGHTS AS A 'LEAST LIKELY' CASE

There are several reasons to expect that the free movement of individuals is a 'least likely' case (Eckstein 1975; Gerring 2007) for a path-dependence explanation. Legally, there is a different set up of the free movement of workers and citizenship rights. Socially, individual actors are concerned, which have much fewer resources in playing a 'Eurolaw game' (Rawlings 1993), while the other freedoms mainly apply to corporate actors. One would therefore expect a different path of legal explanation.

In its wording, the freedom of movement of persons is explicitly linked to non-discrimination, with no equivalence to the prohibition of quantitative restrictions present for goods (Barnard 2001: 38). Different to goods and services, there cannot be a 'double burden' of adhering to the regulations of the home and the host state for natural or legal persons, but an integration into the host state takes place and its rules apply (Barnard 2010: 240). Moreover, the freedom of movement for workers has been shaped much more through secondary law than the other freedoms (Barnard 2010: 240, 224f). The Court therefore had many indications how member states envisaged the interpretation of this freedom.

Different lines of argumentation of the Court with regard to the freedoms resulted.

> In the 1970s and 1980s the prevailing view was that the scope of the four freedoms should be drawn along different lines: Article 28 EC on the free movement of goods was to be considered as a far-reaching prohibition of any measures potentially hindering or restricting the import of goods, whether indistinctly applicable or not. . . . In contrast, the provisions on the free movement of persons – workers, establishment and services – were generally regarded as an expression of the general principle of non-discrimination on grounds of nationality, as set forth in Article 12 EC. (Oliver and Roth 2004: 411)

Also citizenship rights show specificities. As a last minute addition to the Treaty of Maastricht, without significant political discussions (Aziz 2009: 291), EU citizenship supplements national citizenship and the free movement of workers on the European level. All citizens of all member states automatically qualify. EU citizens may move and reside freely throughout the EU, and may stand and vote in elections for municipalities and the European Parliament (Wind 2009: 254). Also relevant is Art. 12 (now Art. 16D) prohibiting discrimination on the ground of nationality.

Next to legal differences, it is questionable whether individuals can act as well as corporate actors as positive feedback for pushing an extensive interpretation along. However, non-governmental organizations (NGOs) play an important role in furthering individual European rights. Well known is the significance of the British Equal Opportunity Office (EOO) in strategically initiating cases that were handed as preliminary procedures to the ECJ (Alter and Vargas 2000). NGOs can play a similar role by linking with law firms. One example is *Watts* (C-372/04), an important case for the freedom of health services, where Ms Watts went abroad to avoid the waiting time for a new hip which the National Health Service imposed. She was supported by the law firm Leigh Day and Co that has strong links to a variety of NGOs[3], and offers its services for free to clients in strategic cases.

Also to be noted in this context is the European Citizen Action Service (ECAS). When citizens access the EU homepage for information on their rights ('Europe Direct'), their questions are answered by the Citizen Signpost Service that is run by ECAS for DG Market. A team of 60 legal experts provides free advice on about 10,000 questions each year.[4] This allows ECAS to pick important cases. Despite a weak legal basis, there could thus be sufficient support for individuals to foster an expansive interpretation.

The development of the case law on workers' free movement

Originally, rights for residence and movement in the EU were strictly tied to being a worker. In the 1980s a series of cases (53/81; 139/85; 196/87) broadened the application, making it sufficient to be economically active at all, not necessarily earning enough for one's living (Davies 2003: 195). The Court largely followed a discriminatory test (Barnard 2001: 38f).

Bosman (C-415/93) brought about a major shift. Here a non-discriminatory rule was declared 'an obstacle to the freedom of movement' (para 103). Thus, with *Bosman* the Court moved to an interpretation of a prohibition of restrictions. As known from goods, this is coupled with the question of public interests ('mandatory requirements'), and proportionality. The restrictions path has by now become the dominant interpretation of the freedom of movement.

> Whatever nomenclature used in that jurisprudence, be it manifested in impeding access/hindrance to trade or the terminology of 'liable to hamper or to render less attractive', it is crucial to appreciate that the common objective in all such jurisprudence is the removal of the restriction to exercise the free movement right. (Connor 2010: 177)

With the change towards a prohibition of restrictions, potentially the Court can classify any national rule as a restriction to a freedom (Barnard 2010: 258), there not being a threshold to the extent of hindrance. However, the Court accepts that member states can require a 'link' to their territory when social benefits are concerned. In *Hartmann* (C-212/05) a family had moved to Austria, thereby losing the German child benefit owing to the residence principle. The Court argued that residence was not the only possible link with the husband being a German civil servant. Interestingly, the Advocate General came to the opposite conclusion (para 88), because the family's movement had been unconnected to employment.

Many conflicts have centred on the question of whether social benefits accrued in one member state are exportable to another. Following regulation 1408/71 social security schemes are exportable, but social assistance remains territorially bound. As benefits cannot always be clearly assigned to one or the other, several court cases ensued (e.g., 139/82; 381/85). Often, the Court rules against the opinions of several member states or against existing secondary law, showing how little the preferences of member states determine its case law (Martinsen and Falkner 2011; Wasserfallen 2010).

The *Ibrahim* (C-310/08) judgment of 23 February 2010 further extended access to social assistance. A Somali woman in the United Kingdom (UK) was granted the right to social assistance given that her children – Danish nationals – were going to school there. Interestingly the legal costs of this landmark ruling were paid by Shelter, a UK charity supporting homeless people, who mandated a large barristers' chambers to argue this case at the ECJ.[5]

The other tendency that has to be noted will also play a role when we turn to citizenship rights. Starting with *d'Hoop* (C-224/98), the Court has argued that measures count as restrictions that make the take up of free movement rights less attractive. D'Hoop was a Belgian whose secondary school education in another member state implied that she could not qualify for the Belgian tideover allowance available to school-leavers. *Hartmann*, discussed above, is also part of this line of cases, as losing child-raising benefits may deter people from taking residence abroad.

Recently, the Court has pushed this interpretation further, arguing not only against restrictions but even requiring member states' support for mobility. *Hendrix* (C-287/05) concerned the Dutch incapacity benefit for young people. Mr Hendrix had moved to Belgium while continuing to work in the Netherlands. The Court challenged the legality of the territoriality principle for social assistance, arguing against the existing social security regulation (1408/71, now 883/04). Consequently, member states have to justify restrictions on the export of benefits, with the proportionality review being a task for the local court. '[T]he development in Hendrix can be seen as a way of facilitating free movement by encouraging the homestate to bear some of the costs of the emigration of its citizens, and not just the host state' (Barnard 2010: 283). Again, the Court expanded the reach of rights against a large body of secondary law. If any disincentives to moving abroad count as restrictions to the free movement of workers, clearly many far-reaching changes become necessary at the member-state level.

The case law on citizenship

Although EU citizenship rights were introduced merely as a supplement, their interpretation has resulted in comprehensive citizen rights, thereby even subsuming the other fundamental freedoms (Davies 2003: 189; but see Wollenschläger 2011: 30). In its case law, the ECJ has incrementally extended rights from workers to economically inactive EU citizens (Menéndez 2009: 16). Furthermore, the language of restrictions is being transferred to citizenship law. *Martinez Sala* (C-85/96) is the first notable case, where citizenship rights implied that an economically inactive Union citizen lawfully residing in Germany had to have access to child benefit as Germans do (Tryfonidou 2010: 39).

In *Grzelcyk* (C-184/99) the Court established a right of residence also for economically inactive Union citizens, here a student, requiring assistance. Only if they are an 'unreasonable burden' can this right be withdrawn; otherwise they have to be treated on a par with nationals regarding social assistance (Tryfonidou 2010: 39). The Court thereby contradicted directive 93/96 that requires students from other member states to have sufficient resources as to avoid needing assistance, and its own case law in *Brown* (197/ 86) (Wind 2009: 258).

The *Grzelcyk* ruling was passed during the negotiations of the citizenship directive (2004/38). In it, the member states largely followed the ECJ's case law, allowing permanent residence and access to all social assistance measures after five years of residence. Within the first five years, citizens are required to be able to support themselves financially. But if social assistance in the host state is being sought, expulsion cannot be an automatic reaction. There needs to be 'an unreasonable burden on the host state' for this to be justifiable, reflecting the Court's argument in the *Grzelczyk* case (Wind 2009: 243).

In *Baumbast* (C-413/99), the Court ruled for the first time that EU citizens enjoy a right of residence and movement by direct application of Art. 18 I, not requiring secondary law (Wind 2009: 256, 259). In *Collins* (C-138/02) the Court argued that the general principle of non-discrimination (Arts. 6, 8) implied rights 'to benefits of financial nature' (para. 50). Moreover, rights of residence given by the member states were seen as merely declaratory, and not as legally constitutive; the right being already 'conferred directly by the Treaty' (para. 40). In *Trojani* (C-456/02), the Court further spelled out how rights to financial benefits grounded in non-discrimination, thus contradicting directive 90/364 (Wind 2009: 243, 260).

De Cuyper (C-406/04) concerned the question of whether the granting of social benefits could be territorially restricted. The Court argued that a disadvantage occurring simply owing to the fact that a national exercised the freedom of movement clearly fell under Art. 18 (para. 39). As before with the freedom of workers (*d'Hoop*), it emphasized that no disadvantage may be suffered from using the free-movement right. In this case, the residence clause was, however, seen to be in the public interest (para. 48).

> The language of *De Cuyper* is similar to that of *Cassis de Dijon*. It is the restrictiveness of the measure which is considered to be egregious, but it will be considered lawful if it is in the public interest and proportionate. (Chalmers and Monti 2008: 127)

Altogether, the case law aligns the rights of workers and non-workers (Wind 2009: 243). Moreover, the case law on citizenship makes inroads into national welfare systems when pursuing non-discrimination. A state can no longer privilege its own nationals. While for goods non-discrimination is much more autonomy-regarding than home-country rule, this is not true for persons. Here, non-discrimination is far-reaching, prohibiting a differentiation between nationals and EU citizens. By coupling citizenship and non-discrimination, the ECJ pursues a perspective of equal rights, making it increasingly unimportant which nationality someone has.

To what extent can we speak of path dependence, however, when the case law follows home-country rule for goods, services, capital and establishment, and – effectively – host-country rule for persons? In all areas, and this is the commonality, we find a development towards a prohibition on restrictions of movement. Such a restriction may consist of not granting equal access to social benefits, or of making the movement of nationals to other member states less attractive.

Having established these broad citizenship rights, the Court's case law subsequently expanded the eligibility to these rights. A few developments shall be summarized before closing. In *Zhu and Chen* (C-200/02), decided in 2004, the Court allowed (Chinese) parents to partake in the citizenship rights of their (Irish-born) child. *Zambrano* (C34/09) extended the reasoning of *Chen* by granting third-country national parents the right of residence and work, as their expulsion would take EU citizenship away from their children born in Belgium. It was a purely internal situation with no cross-border movement. Also *Metock* (C-127/08) shows how quickly developments take place in the case law on Union citizenship. While in *Akrich* (C-109/01, decided in 2003) the ECJ had still argued that the right to accompany a Union citizen depended on the prior legal residence of the third-country national, since *Metock* this is no longer necessary. Moreover, member states' power to expel EU citizens for reasons of public security has been curtailed. The ECJ ruled in C-482/01 (para. 67) and C-50/06 (para. 43) that the public policy restriction regarding illegal activities needs to be interpreted narrowly. *Rottmann* (Case C-135/08) of March 2010 finally shows that member states lose part of their discretion in determining naturalization, having to take into account the concomitant loss of EU citizenship when withdrawing their citizenship.[6]

Some years ago, Kadelbach expected that member states' reaction to the significant broadening of the reach of entitlements to social assistance through the case law would consist of restricting residence rights (Kadelbach 2003: 563). Subsequently, the ECJ has made such a reaction much more difficult. But when member states can no longer restrict eligibility to benefits, they can only cut down on social benefits in general to prevent welfare tourism (Scharpf 2009).

In conclusion, the ECJ has repeatedly deviated from established case law, and from secondary law established by legislative actors. Case law gave litigants incentives to claim European citizenship rights against 'restrictive' member states' provisions, extending the path-dependent interpretation of the fundamental freedoms to this area. As a result, citizenship rights have had an astonishing career from being a rather meaningless Treaty addition to becoming a central tenet of EU law.

CONCLUSION

The ECJ has been, and continues to be, a major force furthering European integration, and its case law on the fundamental freedoms has been very important in this respect. I have argued that based on the coincidence of the early transnationalizing goods markets, an approach of prohibiting restrictions to these fundamental freedoms has been established as a 'path', to which the interpretations of the other freedoms have converged. Focussing on the freedom of workers' and citizenship rights as a crucial case, I have shown how this path was adopted, despite good reasons for the Court to treat these freedoms differently. Once legal issues related to trade do not only touch on the free movement of goods, typically different freedoms are concerned in one case, broadening the path established in the area of free movement of goods to other related freedoms.

I have argued that legal arguments made in one area – goods – can give incentives to private actors to reason analogously for other freedoms. The action of litigants provides positive feedback to the path. The Court may follow the arguments and thereby sets incentives for yet more actors to pursue this route. By not following certain arguments, in contrast, the Court dissuades actors from certain lines of reasoning. The judges, thus, are not bound by precedent and its path. There are, however, positive incentives for the court to honour precedent, as there are to a convergent approach to the interpretation of all fundamental freedoms. The ECJ is highly dependent on the co-operation of the national courts, which apply EU law autonomously, whenever precedent is sufficiently clear and unambiguous, so that a preliminary ruling is not necessary. Too many changes in its case law and a differentiated approach to the different freedoms would complicate and hamper the diffusion of EU law as the 'law of the land'.

The advantage of a path-dependent argument is that it takes the law seriously and provides for an independent role of legal doctrine (Smith 2008). While legal doctrine can be handled with several degrees of freedom by the judges, it provides an important orienting function for litigants. The concept of path dependence allows taking this ideational influence into account. As it stands, the article could only make it plausible that the transfer of a prohibition of restriction to the case law of free movement and citizenship took place via positive feedback of litigants. To be more precise, it would be necessary to show via process-tracing using, for instance, interview data with litigants, how they and their attorneys, possibly aided by NGOs, strategically took up legal arguments as a means to expand rights in other areas. But such a micro-perspective would need the space of a book.

How would one refute that a path-dependent process was taking place? Case law often is ambiguous and where one scholar still sees a non-discrimination approach (Davies 2003), another sees a prohibition of restriction (Barnard 2010), while yet another argues for an evolving market access test (Tryfonidou 2010). Notwithstanding these differences in classification, there is widespread agreement among legal scholars on a convergence in the interpretation of the fundamental freedoms through the ECJ (Barnard 2010; Davies 2003; Oliver and Roth 2004; Tryfonidou 2010). Would there still be distinct reasoning on the different fundamental freedoms, we would not see the identical argumentative figures in different areas, and there would be no path dependence.

Applied to citizenship rights, the language of prohibiting restrictions coupled with the principle of non-discrimination on the basis of nationality has led to a significant broadening of rights of EU citizens, and resulting difficulties of member states to restrict social benefits, and increasingly even of shaping their national citizenship law. As is often the case, the Court invites a balance between European individual rights and national political concerns. However, as each case deals with individuals, it is hardly imaginable that these could pose 'an unreasonable burden' on a member state, be it for its welfare or public security. The actual 'burden' is a cumulative issue. For the Commission and the Court the expansion of individual European rights is a welcome development to bring Europe 'home' to the citizens, to show that integration makes a difference, and thereby to get much needed support.

> Notwithstanding this, the political elite of Europe has mismanaged the EU's constitutional process by failing to place the citizen at the center. . . . The same

> cannot be said regarding the judicial elite, who have championed the cause of citizenship to a considerable extent. (Aziz 2009: 282)

Whether this pays out as planned once citizens realize that there is a concomitant loss of national means to democratically shape the welfare state remains to be seen. Given these dangers to the legitimacy of a court-shaped rights regime, I have argued that the path results in political 'inefficiency'. There are overwhelming arguments that the citizenship rights regime of the EU needs to be politically shaped – and not by the Court (Bellamy 2007).

Biographical note: Susanne K. Schmidt is Professor of Political Science and Dean of the Bremen International Graduate School of Social Sciences at the University of Bremen.

ACKNOWLEDGEMENTS

I would like to thank Philipp Martel, Anna-Lena Lillie, Daniel Kosak and Rike Krämer for research assistance, Jonathan Smiles for English corrections, and Martin Höpner, Yannis Karagiannis and Fritz Scharpf, as well as two anonymous reviewers for comments. Financial support through the German Research Foundation via the CRC 597 is gratefully acknowledged.

NOTES

1 I thank Fritz Scharpf for pointing out the usefulness of this distinction to me.
2 The freedom of capital is a special case but also fits the argument (see Blauberger *et al.* forthcoming, 2012).
3 See http://www.leighday.co.uk/about-us/social-justice (accessed 7 September 2011).
4 ECAS Mind the Gap, report December 2009, p. 16f.
5 http://www.gardencourtchambers.co.uk/news/news_detail.cfm?iNewsID=548 (accessed 7 September 2011).
6 See the discussion by several scholars of the case under http://eudo-citizenship.eu/citizenship-forum/254-has-the-european-court-of-justice-challenged-member-state-sovereignty-in-nationality-law (accessed 7 September 2011).

REFERENCES

Alter, K.J. (2001) *Establishing the Supremacy of European Law – The Making of an International Rule of Law in Europe*, Oxford: Oxford University Press.

Alter, K.J. and Vargas, J. (2000) 'Explaining variation in the use of European litigation strategies: European Community law and British gender equality policy', *Comparative Political Studies* 33(4): 452–82.

Aziz, M. (2009) 'Implementation as the test case of European Union Citizenship', *Columbia Journal of European Law* 15(2): 281–98.

Barnard, C. (2001) 'Fitting the remaining pieces into the goods and persons jigsaw?' *European Law Review* 26(1): 35–59.
Barnard, C. (2010) *The Substantive Law of the EU. The Four Freedoms*, Oxford, New York: Oxford University Press.
Bartels, B.L. (2009) 'The constraining capacity of legal doctrine on the US Supreme Court', *American Political Science Review* 103(3): 474–95.
Bellamy, R. (2007) *Political Constitutionalism: A Republican Defence of the Constitutionality of Democracy*, Cambridge: Cambridge University Press.
Blauberger, M., Krüger, T. and Schmidt, S.K. (forthcoming, 2012) 'Die Pfadabhängigkeit internationaler Verrechtlichung. EU und WTO im Vergleich', *Zeitschrift für Internationale Beziehungen* 19(1).
Chalmers, D. and Monti, G. (2008) *European Union Law: Text and Materials: Updating Supplement*, Cambridge: Cambridge University Press.
Connor, T. (2010) 'Goods, persons, services and capital in the European Union: jurisprudential routes to free movement', *German Law Journal* 11(2): 159–209.
David, P.A. (1985) 'Clio and the economics of QWERTY', *American Economic Review* 75(2): 332–37.
Davies, G. (2003) *Nationality Discrimination in the European Internal Market*, London and New York: Kluwer Law International.
Dyevre, A. (2010) 'Unifying the field of comparative judicial politics: towards a general theory of judicial behaviour', *European Political Science Review* 2(2): 297–327.
Eckstein, H. (1975) 'Case study and theory in political science', in I.G. Fred and N.W. Polsby (eds), *Handbook of Political Science Volume 7*, Reading, MA: Addison-Wesley, pp. 79–137.
Fon, V., Parisi, F. and Depoorter, B. (2005) 'Litigation, judicial path-dependence, and legal change', *European Journal of Law and Economics* 20(1): 43–56.
Garrett, G. (1995) 'The politics of legal integration in the European Union', *International Organization* 49(1): 171–81.
Garrett, G., Kelemen, R.D. and Schulz, H. (1998) 'The European Court of Justice, national governance, and legal integration in the European Union', *International Organization* 52(1): 149–76.
Gely, R. and Spiller, P.T. (2008) 'Strategic judicial decision-making', in K.E. Whittington, R.D. Kelemen and G.A. Caldeira (eds), *The Oxford Handbook of Law and Politics*, Oxford: Oxford University Press, pp. 24–46.
Genschel, P. and Jachtenfuchs, M. (2011) 'How the European Union constrains the state: multilevel governance of taxation', *European Journal of Political Research* 50(3): 293–314.
Gerhardt, M.J. (2005) 'The limited path of dependency of precedent', *Journal of Constitutional Law* 7(4): 903–1000.
Gerring, J. (2007) 'Is there a (viable) crucial-case method?' *Comparative Political Studies* 40(3): 231–53.
Granger, M.-P. (2004) 'When governments go to Luxembourg . . . : the influence of governments on the Court of Justice', *European Law Review* 29(1): 3–31.
Joerges, C. (1996) 'Taking the law seriously: on political science and the role of law in the process of European integration', *European Law Journal* 2(2): 105–35.
Kadelbach, S. (2003) 'Unionsbürgerschaft', in A. von Bogdandy (ed.), *Europäisches Verfassungsrecht: theoretische und dogmatische Grundzüge*, Berlin/Heidelberg: Springer-Verlag, pp. 539–82.
Kelemen, R.D. (2012) 'The political foundations of judicial independence in the European Union', *Journal of European Public Policy* 19(1): 43–58.
Mahoney, J. (2000) 'Path dependence in historical sociology', *Theory and Society* 29(4): 507–48.

Malecki, M. (2012) 'Do ECJ judges all speak with the same voice? Evidence of divergent preferences from the judgments of chambers', *Journal of European Public Policy* 19(1): 59–75.
Martinsen, D.S. and Falkner, G. (2011) 'Social policy: problem-solving gaps, partial exits and court-decision traps', in G. Falkner (ed.), *The EU's Decision Traps: Comparing Policies*, Oxford: Oxford University Press, pp. 128–44.
McCall Smith, J. (2000) 'The politics of dispute settlement design: explaining legalism in regional trade pacts', *International Organization* 54(1): 137–80.
McCown, M. (2003) 'The European Parliament before the bench: ECJ precedent and EP litigation strategies', *Journal of European Public Policy* 10(6): 974–95.
Menéndez, A.J. (2009) 'European Citizenship after *Martinez Sala* and *Baumbast*: has European law become more human and less social?', *RECON Online Working Paper 2009/05*.
Oliver, P. and Roth, W.-H. (2004) 'The internal market and the four freedoms', *Common Market Law Review* 41(2): 407–41.
Pierson, P. (2000) 'Increasing returns, path dependence, and the study of politics', *American Political Science Review* 94(2): 251–67.
Rawlings, R. (1993) 'The Eurolaw game: some deductions from a saga', *Journal of Law and Society* 20(3): 309–40.
Scharpf, F.W. (2009) 'Legitimacy in the multilevel European polity', *European Political Science Review* 1(2): 173–204.
Schmidt, S.K. (2009) 'When efficiency results in redistribution: the conflict over the single services market', *West European Politics* 32(4): 847–65.
Smith, R.M. (2008) 'Historical institutionalism and the study of law', in K.E. Whittington, R.D. Kelemen and G.A. Caldeira (eds), *The Oxford Handbook of Law and Politics*, Oxford: Oxford University Press, pp. 46–63.
Stone Sweet, A. (2002) 'Path dependence, precedent, and judicial power', in M. Shapiro and A. Stone Sweet (eds), *On Law, Politics, and Judicialization*, Oxford and New York: Oxford University Press, pp. 112–35.
Stone Sweet, A. (2010) 'The European Court of Justice and the judicialization of EU governance', *Living Reviews in European Governance* 5(2): 1–50.
Stone Sweet, A. and Brunell, T.L. (2008) 'Note on the data sets: litigating EU law under the Treaty of Rome', *Report of the New Modes of Governance Project no. CIT1-CT-2004-506392*, Florence: European University Institute.
Sun, J.-M. and Pelkmans, J. (1995) 'Regulatory competition in the single market', *Journal of Common Market Studies* 33(1): 67–89.
Tryfonidou, A. (2010) 'Further steps on the road to convergence among the market freedoms', *European Law Review* 35(1): 1–20.
Wasserfallen, F. (2010) 'The judiciary as legislator? How the European Court of Justice shapes policy-making in the European Union', *Journal of European Public Policy* 17(8): 1128–46.
Wind, M. (2009) 'Post-national citizenship in Europe: the EU as a "welfare rights generator"?', *The Columbia Journal of European Law* 15(2): 239–64.
Wollenschläger, F. (2011) 'A new fundamental freedom beyond market integration: Union citizenship and its dynamics for shifting the economic paradigm of European integration', *European Law Journal* 17(1): 1–34.

The reference points of EU judicial politics

Damian Chalmers and Mariana Chaves

ABSTRACT Explanations of the dynamics of EU judicial politics must also account for its incidence. Incidence relies on a relationship between three arenas – those for norm-setting, litigation and judgments – with each conditioning the possibilities for action in the others. Through a study of all 2007–2009 preliminary rulings we find two predominant dynamics here. 'Patrol norms' dedicated to securing common policies give rise to low salience judgments dominated by transnational enterprise and national administration litigation. 'Thickly evaluative norms' are concerned with articulating certain values. Dominated by litigation by domestic undertakings and non-commercial actors, these norms generate the Court's most salient judgments.

INTRODUCTION

Most recent accounts accept that no single narrative fully explains European Union (EU) judicial politics (Alter 2009: 22–5; Jupille and Caporaso 2009; Kelemen 2011: 39f.). Research will accordingly need to consider the conditions under which one narrative holds rather than another. Comparison of patterns of litigation or adjudication across sectors or from different territories will go some way towards answering this. However, any comparison will also have to include analysis of the incidence of EU judicial politics, namely when and where it takes place. For the decision to enact a norm susceptible to judicial politics, to litigate or to refer a matter to the Court always involves a choice when other alternatives are available, and these choices set the conditions for judicial politics. Acceptance of such a relationship between the incidence and dynamics of EU judicial politics has two immediate implications. First, it necessarily problematizes the incidence of EU judicial politics. As we shall see, very few EU legal norms are susceptible to the traditionally understood form of judicial politics which emerges from national courts and ascends to the Court of Justice. Adjudication rates between EU legal sectors vary significantly (Chalmers 2000: 179) and litigation patterns are often significantly affected by external unpredictable factors (Cichowski 2007: 32–4). Thinking about incidence not only helps us with the determinants of EU judicial politics but also informs us about the nature of the judicial beast. Secondly, it goes to the scope of inquiry. Any research into EU judicial politics must analyse the relationship between the adjudicated legal norm, the litigants/referring court and the decision of the Court itself as each is a pre-condition for the presence of the other. Neither the dynamics nor incidence of EU judicial politics can, thus, be considered without analysis of all three of these elements.

By analysing all preliminary rulings given in 2007–2009 through the lens of this relationship we find EU judicial politics to be sectorally confined, highly institutionally autonomous and, in many ways, characterized by a different mission from other parts of the integration process. It is, furthermore, dominated by two dynamics. The first is where the EU law-maker enlists the judiciary's help to secure common policies, typically those of the regulatory state. It is deployed to ensure the main protagonists meet their commitments to one another. Litigation is dominated by constituencies influential in the law-making process and judgments tend not to be salient as the judicial role is about policing these commitments and finessing differences between these constituencies. The other is where EU legal instruments orient themselves more exclusively to the allocation of values rather than to securing common policies. These instruments are much rarer but generate a dynamic dominated by recursive case law and litigants, be they small industry or non-commercial actors, who are both domestic and enjoy traditionally limited influence within the law-making process. It is the bringing of the Court of Justice into this peculiar admixture of domestic disagreement, value iconography and redrawing of the boundaries of élite competition within this second process that has given the Court of Justice its prominence.

THE ARENAS OF EU JUDICIAL POLITICS

The litigated norm, the identity of the litigant and the judgment itself are each indispensable to EU judicial politics. The litigated norm determines the level and form of judicial involvement and the Court's relationship with different constituencies. The litigants (and referring courts) provide the demand for judgments, frame the questions asked of the Court and provide expertise to the Court in the form of legal arguments and evidence as to how legal norms are experienced. The judgment is determinative of the dispute and constrains litigants and law-makers. Their interdependence leads to EU judicial politics being played out as a series of sequential interactions in three arenas:

- The decision by the law-maker, be it Treaty framer or Union legislature, to enact norms susceptible to judicial politics;[1]
- The decision by parties to litigate and to involve the Court of Justice through seeking a preliminary reference;
- The judicial decision itself.

Within these arenas, the relationship structures interactions in three ways. First, with the exception of the initial law-maker, *prior outcomes* from one arena structure possibilities in the other arenas. Second, most actors must factor into their decision-making a *calculus of legal risk* which anticipates responses to their decisions not only in the current arena but in the other two arenas. Judgments may provoke possible undesirable legal reforms or vexatious litigation. New laws may generate undesirable patterns of litigation and opportunities for judicial activism. Reckless litigation may induce legislative and judicial responses depriving litigants of current benefits. Third, as decision-making in each arena can never take place simultaneously with decision-making in other arenas, the mixture of prior outcomes and legal risk facing parties in each arena will always be different.

The calculus of choice for parties is not an abstract one. It is informed by the formal procedures set out in the Treaty on European Union (TEU) which constrain possibilities and set out incentive structures. The preliminary reference procedure in Article 267 Treaty on the Functioning of the European Union (TFEU) is, in this regard, the epicentre of EU judicial politics. It and the enforcement procedure accounted in 2009 for 87.8 per cent of the judgments delivered by the Court with it accounting for 49.9 per cent (European Court of Justice 2010: 87). It places the Court of Justice at the forefront of the decision-making process and involves a wider range of constituencies as references emerge from litigation involving potentially any kind of party before any style of Union court or tribunal, with the latter often seeking expertise on issues where there is no consensus about the content of EU law. By contrast, enforcement procedures against member states are preceded by lengthy Commission–member state negotiations with only a small proportion (in 2009 about 4 per cent) reaching judgment (European Commission 2010: 3). It is thus an arena of dispute settlement of last resort with the Commission winning 92.7 per cent of the cases in 2005–2009 (European Court of Justice 2010: 93). This leads to more salient and controversial issues being decided more frequently under the preliminary reference procedure. Thus, 73 per cent of the judgments cited as significant during the period by the Court in its Annual Reports were preliminary rulings (European Court of Justice 2008: 11–50, 2009: 11–53, 2010: 11–53).

The remainder of this contribution looks at how these interactions are played out through an analysis of all preliminary rulings given by the Court of Justice in the years 2007–2009. There were 549 judgments generating 8981 observations. Sufficiently after the completion of the area of freedom, security and justice and the 2004 enlargements for possible effects to be felt on the case law, the period is also sufficiently proximate to obtain reliable socio-economic data about the composition of the litigants.

THE EU LAW-MAKER AND THE REMIT OF THE JUDICIAL GAME

Judicial politics a confined and unrepresentative form of integration

EU law-makers have a choice whether or not to include justiciable entitlements that can be invoked in domestic courts and subject to Article 267 TFEU in their laws. The risk is that judges and litigants will interpret and apply these in ways that deviate from their preferences. Benefits are potentially two-fold. First, in the case of realization of common goods and policies, judicial enforcement can help secure credibility of legislative commitments, which is, in turn, seen as necessary to prevent free-riding and as a precondition for policy effectiveness. Second, it can be used to institutionalize value-commitments which are articulated as deeply held but are set out only generally in legal documents because of uncertainty and veiled disagreement as to their scope (e.g., civil liberties, liberal market values). The two roles are distinct. The former is concerned with the judiciary contributing to realizing a densely institutionalized common policy as one cog in a wider settlement. With the latter, the judiciary is deployed to reinforce certain belief-systems and to deter egregious behaviour by increasing the costs of violation – be this financially or by naming and shaming (Howse and Teitel 2010: 131). The former is more prevalent in the EU. Its centre of gravity is still that of the regulatory state with little explicit role for in the direct allocation of values. EU law-makers' interest in the judiciary is, thus, largely concerned with its first role of contributing to common goods rather than its latter one of reinforcing certain belief-systems.

The first implication is that EU law-makers would only exceptionally be interested in granting justiciable entitlements subject to Article 267 TFEU. A substitute procedure, the Article 258 TFEU enforcement procedure, secures legal commitments sufficiently effectively. Far more infringements, 2,900 in 2009 (European Commission 2010: 3), are investigated than references made under Article 267 TFEU, 302 in 2009 (European Court of Justice 2010: 82). Compliance rates are reasonably high (Börzel 2001). It also carries less risk as it does not enfranchise new actors, such as domestic courts or litigants, with unpredictable preferences.

The rulings in this period reflect this. There are, according to the Court of Justice, 49 fields of legislative activity. During this period there were preliminary rulings in 35 of them. However, Table 1 illustrates that the number of rulings in most was minimal. In only 13 fields were there more than 15 judgments – a threshold of one reference for every 5.4 member states per year. The situation is even more concentrated when one looks at where litigation is clustered. If the economic freedoms are placed together on the grounds that these are represented by single provisions in other jurisdictions (e.g., the commerce clause in the United States) and the common customs tariff and customs union are treated as a tax, over 80 per cent of case law was in seven fields: the economic freedoms; harmonization of laws; taxation; freedom; security and justice; environment; agriculture and social policy.

Second, member states taking risks through significant steps in the integration process (e.g., accession, new EU competencies, ambitious Action Plans) would rarely wish to generate further volatility by allowing unpredictable constituencies to manage expectations over these through the preliminary reference procedure. This leads to little direct link between judicial integration and the integration process more generally. References are, thus, very stable across

Table 1 Sectors, litigants and significant judgments

		Identity of litigants %					Significant judgments	
Area of Law	*Number of cases per field*	*Domestic firms*	*Multinationals*	*State*	*Individuals*	*Others*	*Number*	*%*
Taxation	87	24	17	51	6	3	6	6.90
Agriculture	45	34	7	44	11	4	4	8.89
Approximation of laws	41	32	27	21	13	6	13	31.71
Social policy	33	13	7	32	41	6	16	48.48
Environment & consumers	32	19	11	41	19	11	11	34.38
Area of freedom, security and justice	27	27	11	13	45	5	9	33.33
Customs custom tariff	26	28	19	49	4	0	0	0
Free movement of persons	26	8	2	44	42	4	11	42.31
Freedom to provide services	22	23	9	45	14	9	11	50
Free movement of capital	21	19	7	50	24	0	8	38.10
Freedom of establishment	20	20	12	44	15	10	10	50
Law relating to undertakings	17	49	0	40	3	9	5	29.41
Free movement of goods	16	36	9	33	12	10	8	50
Competition	12	29	25	21	4	21	6	50
Customs Union	12	21	29	46	4	0	1	8.33
Industrial policy	12	27	23	38	4	8	2	16.67

(*Continued*)

Table 1 Continued

		Identity of litigants %					*Significant judgments*	
Area of Law	*Number of cases per field*	*Domestic firms*	*Multinationals*	*State*	*Individuals*	*Others*	*Number*	*%*
External relations	11	9	5	45	41	0	4	36.36
Policing and judicial cooperation in criminal matters	11	0	0	41	50	9	6	54.55
Social security for migrant workers	11	5	0	50	45	0	2	18.18
Intellectual property	10	30	45	5	5	15	5	50

Note: A large number of the titles are cryptic. 'Industrial policy' involves judgments on harmonization of legislation on network industries; 'Law of Undertakings' concerns EU public procurement law; 'External Relations' involved association or neighbourhood agreements with non-EU states and invariably focussed on the rights of non-EU migrants under these.

time, notwithstanding other developments in the integration process. The pattern of references set out in Table 1 follows an almost identical pattern to that of Brunell *et al.* (2008) in their work on preliminary rulings up to 2006, with the sole exception of the emergence of the area of freedom, security and justice as a significant field of referral. Significant legislative programmes such as the 1992 programme or the Financial Services Action Programme do not lead to corresponding surges in referrals. In the case of the 1992 programme, Brunell *et al.* (2008: 27) discovered that references moved from about 3.8 per cent of references in the late 1980s to 7.7 per cent of references by the end of the 1990s, but this still accounted for only about 30 references per year or, put another way, two per year from each member state. Similarly, the accession of the 10 member states in 2004 has not yet led to an increase in preliminary rulings – with 254 in 2005 and 259 in 2009 (European Court of Justice 2010: 86).[2] Furthermore, there has been pre-emption of the preliminary reference procedure where a new field was anticipated to generate large numbers of references. Most notably, the establishment of the area of freedom, security and justice (AFSJ) at the Treaty of Amsterdam was accompanied by a limiting of the preliminary reference procedure to member states who chose to opt in for policing and judicial co-operation in criminal matters (PJCCM; Art. 35 TEU) and a confining of the power to refer to courts against whose decisions there was no judicial remedy for all other matters connected to AFSJ (Art. 68 TEU). These restrictions were only abolished by the Treaty of Lisbon.

The norms of judicial politics: patrol norms and thickly evaluative norms

If law-makers only deploy the preliminary reference procedure when it offers comparative institutional advantages, this begs the question what sort of justiciable entitlement would confer such advantage. There are two: patrol norms and thickly evaluative norms.[3] These norms are archetypes and can overlap in different sectors or be present even in a single piece of legislation. Nevertheless, they have sufficiently distinct roles and sufficiently dominant dynamics to be treated autonomously.

Patrol Norms

Actors dominant in the law-making process have no interest in the provision of entitlements allowing others to undermine their interests through litigation. However, most cannot rely on the centralized enforcement procedure to secure their interests insofar as the Commission has discretion over the use of this procedure. There is therefore an interest in entitlements which allow additional patrolling of commitments and the finessing of entitlements as preferences evolve (patrol norms). Examples would be market access rights, rights of due process, rights to challenge administrative decisions which prohibit activity, tax, or refuse to grant financial entitlements. These are likely to be more prevalent in those sectors where deviance generates significant costs for other constituencies – be it denial of market access, significant distortions of competition between undertakings as a result of uneven application of regulatory burdens, illegal taxation or a failure to distribute financial entitlements – as these provide a motivation for patrol. Consequently, patrol norms are confined to EU secondary legislation as the EU Treaties are framework treaties with few precise commitments with identifiable externalities to be patrolled. This is in stark contrast to sectors dominated by detailed legislation with precise commitments, notably the single market, agriculture, taxation, environment and consumer policy, and the area of freedom, security and justice insofar as it applies to judicial co-operation in civil matters.

Patrol norms are more closely associated with the first judicial role identified of securing common policies and the prevention of free-riding and institutionalization of collective action necessary for these. However, to prevent disturbance of the legislative equilibrium the law-maker only grants such norms in narrowly confined circumstances and where their predominant utility is to parties dominant in the law-making process. Looking at Table 1, one would expect them to account for most of the litigation in the single market (approximation of laws, industrial policy and law of undertakings), agriculture, taxation (including customs union and common customs tariff) and some of the environmental litigation. If one includes all environmental and consumer rulings these sectors account for at best 295 judgments during the period. This is over half of the case law analysed, and therefore a predominant part of the Court's work. However, it is dwarfed by the respective legislation in the sectors. The three single market headings comprised, according to EUR-LEX, a total of 1,417 Regulations and Directives; Environment 992 such instruments, and Agriculture 5,285. Referrals are, thus, very much the exception with the single market and agriculture averaging one ruling per 20 and 117 pieces of legislation respectively during the period.

Thickly evaluative norms

These are value-laden norms whose meaning and evaluative resonance cannot be understood in any strong way separately from the factual contexts in which they arise (Penner 2003). An example is discrimination. It is impossible to explain why offering an advantage to one party over another is egregious without placing it in a context which indicates why it is so. These norms challenge the balance about ethical commitments in most laws whereby the latter are only articulated at a certain generality allowing consensus to be maintained where there is deep disagreement. With thickly evaluative norms their heavy reliance on context entails that the initial legal commitments are too vague whilst implementation, by virtue of its being where the action takes place, is highly charged. Courts are thus, typically, deployed first, because they receive information later than the law-maker and are thereby better placed to consider the consequences of different applications of the norm (Rogers 2001). Second, judicial reasoning is well suited to thick evaluation as it is based on an application of norms to factual situations and consideration of the wider implications of this. Third, the parameters of the dispute allow different parties to plead that the ambiguity concealing disagreement is not resolved beyond the factual scenario at the heart of the dispute.

Thickly evaluative norms are more closely associated with the second role of the judiciary, the entrenching of certain belief-systems. They can be present in all sectors as no sector is either value-free or unmarked by deep contingency. They are, however, prevalent in sectors oriented exclusively around Treaty provisions (economic freedoms, competition, economic opportunities), as these provisions set out values to be realized rather than detailed programmes of action. They are also present in sectors more explicitly concerned with the allocation of values – be they AFSJ and PJCCM insofar as they raise civil liberties and public order concerns, and much labour, environmental and consumer protection legislation insofar as they have resort to notions of fairness (labour or consumer law) or precaution (environmental law). These sectors all feature heavily in Table 1.

The prevalence of thickly evaluative norms is even more striking when one looks at the instruments deployed in the rulings. Regulations should be the most referred instrument. At the end of 2009, according to EUR-LEX, there were 7,717 Regulations in force and 1,918 Directives; the circumstances in which Directives can be invoked in domestic courts are more constrained (Chalmers *et al.* 2010: 285–93); and Directives are deployed often because of the sensitivity of their content so there are higher political risks to judicial adventurism. However, the concern that it is problematic to resolve too much which leads member states to agree Directives and Treaty provisions is the same as that which generates thickly evaluative legal norms.

Table 2 shows, therefore, that Directives account for 58 per cent of the secondary legislation invoked in references whilst Regulations account for only 33 per cent. A Directive is 6.7 times more likely to be referred than a Regulation. Similarly, Treaty provisions account for 30 per cent of all referred cases, notwithstanding that, with the exception of Article 63 TFEU,[4] all directly effective provisions date back to the original Treaty of Rome.

LITIGANTS' DEPLOYMENT OF THE PRELIMINARY REFERENCE PROCEDURE

Although national courts formally make the references to the Court of Justice, often the reference will have been drafted by the litigants, and it is highly unusual, other than in criminal cases, for a national court to refer without one litigant pushing for it. Without such demand, the parties will simply settle, thereby taking the matter out of the hands of the courts.[5] National courts have, thus, to be seen as gatekeepers in the process responding to litigant demand. Demand for references will only exist where one party wishes to reorient the legal settlement rather than make other choices such as asking the local

Table 2 Legal instruments (%)

Type of law	*2007*	*2008*	*2009*	*2007–2009*
Secondary	50	78	83	70
Primary	50	22	17	30
Types of secondary law				
Directive	57	63	55	58
Regulation	33	27	40	33
Other	6	4	2	4
Framework decision	2	3	1	2
Convention	2	2	2	2
Decision	0	1	1	1
Type of dispute				
Domestic	64	60	60	62
Transnational	35	40	39	38

court to apply EU law locally or looking for solutions which do not involve EU law. The comparative advantage of this choice will be governed by the relative return offered to litigants by the preliminary reference procedure compared to other institutional alternatives. Its value is less for parties with a wide variety of other avenues at their disposal for securing their preferences. By contrast, rulings become more attractive for parties marginalized within other venues (Alter and Vargas 2000; Slagter 2009). The value increases yet further if the reference opens up opportunity structures for parties where none existed before (Alter 2009; Cichowski 2007).

The preliminary reference procedure has three features which bear upon the litigants' calculation of advantage. It is *time-consuming.* The average period between the reference and Court of Justice judgment at the end of 2009 was 17.1 months (European Court of Justice 2010: 94), to which must be added time spent in the domestic legal system. This makes it ill-suited for those damaged by delay, e.g., those needing quick financial compensation or wishing to protect a market position. However, delay allows its use as a litigation strategy to weaken another litigant's position or to secure injunctive relief from a disliked domestic law, thus allowing the litigant a period of grace from the law pending resolution of the dispute (Rawlings 1993). This benefits actors with interests exclusively in one state as any injunctive relief will fully protect their position as it will apply across the whole of their market, the national territory. Second, the procedure is *expensive.* For those seeking only financial compensation, the returns have to be significant, therefore, to seek a referral. However, these returns may be calculated not simply in terms of the dispute in question but also in terms of opportunity costs. Parties with ongoing relations governed by EU law have therefore a bigger interest in a reference than those in a one-off transaction. Finally, as a preliminary ruling resettles the legal settlement, it attracts those who *litigate to change the law to meet ideological preferences.* Litigation offers high returns here as it does not require litigants to negotiate with other constituencies. Judgments of the Court of Justice are almost never overturned, and, in terms of profile for the litigants and entrenching particular belief-systems, rulings govern a large territory of nearly half a billion people.

This article looked at litigants in the different sectors, whether they were transnational or commercial actors, national administrations, private individuals or 'other actors', who were non-commercial actors, most notably non-governmental organizations (NGOs). Every judgment involves at least two parties and more where cases have been joined. A significant majority of the disputes, 62 per cent, involved litigants who were exclusively domestic (Table 2). In addition, the figures have to be read carefully. Many individuals are supported by NGOs, but this is often difficult to identify, so there is some substitutability here. In addition, there is an over-representation of the state insofar as often it is the body against whom an EU law action must be brought.

Patrol norms and their constituencies

Insofar as patrol norms typically benefit constituencies dominant in the law-making process, it makes sense to analyse the take-up of references by the two parties most regularly dominant in the EU legislative process, transnational enterprises and national administrations. The value of the process is reduced for these by the possibility of institutional substitutes to secure their preferences – be it legislative amendment or, in the case of transnational enterprises, various forms of alternative dispute settlement. In the light of this and the financial and temporal costs of a reference, there seem only two circumstances when there is an incentive to seek a reference. The first is where one of these actors finds no institutional substitute available and the law is sufficiently entrenched, costly and distant from its preferences. The second is where there is no institutional substitute available and the actor is in an ongoing relationship with other actors (e.g., national regulatory or fiscal authorities). In such circumstances, the costs of the reference can seem cheap in relation to the potential indefinite costs suffered from the misaligned law.

Table 1 shows that litigation by transnationals is concentrated in the single market (approximation of laws, industrial policy and intellectual property) and fiscal fields (taxation, customs union and common customs tariff). The incidence is in all cases significant with transnationals accounting for 35 per cent of non-state parties. It is impossible to argue that this is because these sectors are transnational in nature. Taxation, for example, largely concerns value added tax (VAT), a tax governing a far larger proportion of economic activity than transnational trade. Instead, the pattern of litigation fits the thesis of a transnational society which generates its own transnational rules of the game and systems of dispute settlement which are then policed by transnational actors (e.g., Fligstein 2008; Fligstein and McNichol 1998; Stone Sweet and Caporaso 1998;). However, the data also shows the limits of the transnational society thesis. Even in sectors where transnational actors are prevalent, they rarely predominate. The generalizability of legal entitlements enables other actors to invoke them and has given rise to a significant parallel dynamic in most of these sectors in which local industry litigates these norms domestically. However, the most telling limitation is the low levels of transnational litigation. Notwithstanding over 1,400 pieces of legislation, the single market accounted for only 21 referrals per year, of which transnationals comprised about one-quarter of the litigating parties. It is simply something that is rarely used.

The involvement of national administrations is high in almost all sectors. In large part, this is because the state is necessarily the target of EU litigation. However, as defendants, national administrations could always settle if they did not wish a referral. Moreover, it cannot be excluded that they provoke them. If a national administration wants to reorient the legal settlement within its territory, it may regulate or tax at the perimeters of the formal competencies granted by EU law in order to align it with its domestic preferences. This would most likely trigger a reference where it imposes significant costs or sufficiently restricts opportunities for that state's subjects. In such circumstances, both constituencies have an interest in the ruling. The administration wishes to secure legal certainty for a new prerogative, whilst parties subject to an on-going long-term fiscal or regulatory relationship with the administration can see unending costs unless they secure a favourable ruling.

Table 1 shows, therefore, that national administration involvement is over 40 per cent in sectors where EU law has extended national regulatory, fiscal and penal capacities – be this environment law (Andersen and Liefferink 1997: 10–35; Héritier *et al.* 1996), VAT in the field of taxation (Terra and Wattel 2008: 120) or penal law (Chaves 2011: ch. 4). It is also high where EU law grants the state most control over private activities – be it be the extraction or grant of resources to individuals (agriculture, taxation), entry or expulsion of the territory (external relations, free movement of persons), removal of liberty (PJCCM) or significant and costly regulation (environment and consumers). By contrast, it is surprisingly low in fields where the administration would seem the natural defendant (approximation of laws, AFSJ, free movement of goods) but these qualities are not present.

Thickly evaluative norms and their constituencies

As thickly evaluative norms concern situations whose dimensions are difficult to anticipate, their use is rarely confined to a limited range of litigants. This brings two types of litigant into the process largely absent from the referral of patrol norms: those wishing to use litigation to change the general legal settlement for ideological reasons; and domestic traders wishing to use EU law to suspend – initially through interim relief and then through a ruling – a disliked national law. In both instances, the value of the procedure is increased by the possible unavailability of institutional substitutes, as there are strong possibilities that neither will have significant influence in either the domestic or EU law-making processes. However, alongside this, one would expect a slight under-representation from those constituencies who are the targets of the norms in question. These might be unhappy with the EU legal norms, but as their unhappiness is with EU law not domestic law, there is no easy possibility of interim relief. A referral, thus, brings no immediate relief for them but is a costly exercise with the risk that the Court will not accede to their preferences but will provide a ruling that exacerbates the situation.

Table 1 shows sectors characterized by thickly evaluative norms – the economic freedoms, competition, social policy, environment and consumer policy, AFSJ – are all marked by litigant diversity. This cannot be explained by reference to affinities of the sector. Competition, free movement of services and freedom of establishment all require, in principle, the presence or imminence of transnational trade for their instigation. Yet, in all cases, domestic enterprise litigation is higher than that of transnationals. All these fields are also marked by high numbers of domestic litigants – be they commercial or non-commercial. They are thus deployed in disputes which are highly local in substance and go, in the first place, to revision the domestic polity. There is, furthermore, high litigant diversity in all these sectors, including the economic freedoms. Litigation has moved these away from being simply market provisions to the point where they are being deployed by non-commercial actors to secure broader entitlements from domestic administrations. Finally, there is the under-representation of certain classes of litigant who are disadvantaged by the reference procedure. Two sectors, Social Policy and Environment and Consumer, are characterized by low commercial activity, notwithstanding that these will often be defendants and will bear the brunt of aggressively expanding equal opportunities or consumer protection law.

PRELIMINARY RULINGS AND THE JUDICIAL DECISION

The Court's interest in its judgments is to secure authority for itself and its work. However, there are a wide variety of constituencies it has to satisfy. To be sure, this includes litigants and governments. It is, thus, more likely to accept a point argued by a greater number of states or by parties privy to the dispute (Carrubba *et al.* 2008; Granger 2004). More general literature on courts suggests reputation within legal and judicial peer communities weighs particularly heavily on these (Miceli and Coşgel 1994; Schauer 2000). The views of senior courts and legal specialists matter (Alter 2009: 63ff; Schepel and Wesseling 1997; Stein 1981). However, courts' wider authority with their subjects is dependent on their arguments appearing to be legally rather than politically reasoned (Gibson *et al.* 2005). There is, thus, a premium in making arguments perceived by these constituencies as legally appropriate, intellectually cogent and principled. Prior case law weighs particularly heavily on the decision-making of the Court (Komárek 2011: ch. 6 and 7).

To mediate between these interests in a legally reasoned manner, the Court adopts particular roles in relation to types of dispute. These provide a template which settles other parties' expectations of what the Court will do and what they can ask of it. They also allow the Court some autonomy as it does not have to make the case anew each time. The role of the Court is shaped, in the first place, by what norms it is asked to adjudicate and, in the second place, by whom it is asked to adjudicate these norms, namely the parties in the dispute and significantly affected third parties.

Disputes involving patrol norms invariably regard challenges to the exercise of regulatory, fiscal and penal capacities by national administrations on the basis that these have breached very specific commitments rather than any deep-seated values. This typically calls the Court into two types of role. The first, that of welfare constitutionalism, asks courts to contribute towards helping government to secure collective goods set out or respected by EU law (i.e., regulation of externalities, collection of taxes, security). This role may involve redirecting other arms of government, but there is a concern not to disrupt the provision of these goods or subvert the institutional processes realizing these (Barber 2003; Murphy 2007). The second role derives from the Court having to secure respect for the patrol norms. This typically brings into play a balancing role in which the Court seeks to ensure that neither the litigated interests nor the public good in question are unduly prejudiced. Neither role calls for the Court to make judgments with a high salience. It is not asked to develop strong autonomous lines of case law or to mark out a striking judicial position which has wider social, economic or political consequences. Furthermore, the nature of patrol norms is that they impose obligations and entitlements on a limited range of parties, so only a small number will be directly affected by a judgment (Chalmers *et al.* 2010: 285–312).

With thickly evaluative norms, the wider variety of parties privy to disputes pushes the Court to have a more strongly assertive role. Litigation by a wide range of constituencies can have destabilizing effects on the law, as a cacophony of voices all claim it means different things unless the Court establishes a strong line of case law which is sufficiently clear to align preferences. There are further pressures. Often such norms also serve to protect diffuse interests which are traditionally poorly served by majoritarian institutions (e.g., minorities, women, consumers, the environment, foreign traders or poorly organized commercial interests). This leads to both an absence of detailed legislative direction and to arguments for a stronger judicial role to rectify this representative deficit on the basis not only that this is desirable (Maduro 1998) but that it is a feature of judicial tradition and one of the bases for public support for the judiciary (Friedman 2003; Vanberg 2001).

One would therefore expect sectors dominated by thickly evaluative norms to give rise to a higher percentage of significant judgments than those dominated by patrol norms. Table 1 suggests that sectors characterized by such norms tend to give rise to more salient judgments. All the economic freedoms, other than free movement of capital, and competition have 40 per cent or more of their rulings characterized as significant. Sectors governed by EU secondary legislation move along a scale. At one end are two sectors, social policy and

PJCCM, heavily informed by thickly evaluative norms for which 48 per cent and 55 per cent of their judgments are deemed significant during this period. There are, then, a number of sectors – approximation of laws, industrial policy and environment and consumers – where about one-third of the rulings are deemed significant. These are sectors where issues of mutual commitment, and thus patrol norms, are prevalent. However, regulatory or fundamental rights norms arise which are thickly evaluative in nature, politically salient, and generate interpretive uncertainty to be resolved by judges. Finally, there are those sectors, taxation and agriculture, dominated by patrol norms with few thickly evaluative norms which have very low percentages of significant rulings.

There is, however, a further reason for the distinction in salience, and this goes to the feedback dynamics surrounding Court judgments. The sectors (economic freedoms, competition, intellectual property, social policy) in which there are the highest proportion of significant judgments are also those characterized by heavy lines of case law. This is paradoxical, as one would expect prior rulings would limit the scope for significant subsequent rulings which would simply follow in their footsteps.

However, with patrol norms, the presence of institutional substitutes for the affected constituencies means that, irrespective of the voting requirements in the Council, there is frequent legislative revision of adjudicated instruments. The centrepiece of EU tax law litigation, the Sixth VAT Directive, was, for example, prior to its recasting in 2006, revised 31 times in its 30 years.[6] Such a shifting legal settlement relativizes the importance of any judgment and also increases the possibility of legislative over-rule.

As thickly evaluative norms enfranchise or adversely affect a wide number of constituencies, judgments touch more directly many more parties not privy to the dispute. For many of these the relative return of preliminary references is high as there are few institutional substitutes for securing their preferences. Even if the original constituencies are satisfied with the new legal settlement set out in a judgment, these 'new entrants' who are now possibly empowered by it will wish to now use the reference procedure that more fully secures their preferences. The referral process, thus, generates its own feedback loops where case law leads to further litigation which in turn provokes more rulings, and so on. However, in each case as it was new constituencies making their own demands, these were often quite significant in political–economic terms.

CONCLUSION

The dual dynamics of patrol norms and thickly evaluative norms reveals both the significance and challenges of both the Court of Justice and EU law. The low salience of patrol norms and their use by a narrow range of constituencies raises issues about the plurality of the judicial process and whether it is being deployed with sufficient rigour. Thickly evaluative norms explain the salience of the Court of Justice. They draw it into the allocation of values and amplification of beliefs in charged circumstances that are simultaneously strongly embedded in local contexts and ones that local settlements have been unable to resolve consensually. However, they occur in sectors which represent a small proportion of total EU law, are institutionally distinct from the other processes of EU law and constitute a very different quality of integration from the rest of the EU institutional settlement, namely securing belief systems rather than realizing common policy. Even if the Union were to have such a role, this still begs the question why it is the Court of Justice that should have a monopoly over this, and whether, if we started anew, the central values we should wish the Union to secure are an *ad hoc* mixture of economic liberalism, equal opportunities and labour rights.

Biographical notes: Professor Damian Chalmers is Professor of European Union Law at the London School of Economics and Political Science. Mariana Chaves is a PhD candidate in European Union Law at the London School of Economics and Political Science.

ACKNOWLEDGEMENTS

We wish to thank Alison Johnston for all her help.

NOTES

1 Law-maker is used to refer to both Treaty framing and secondary legislation in the rest of this article.
2 The rulings given in 2005 were all given on references made before the date of accession. It is thus the most reliable date for comparing pre- and post-accession patterns.
3 Litigants are also given powers to challenge abuse by EU Institutions or significant regulatory or administrative powers before the General Court (e.g. competition and intellectual property). On litigant composition here see Harding and Gibbs (2005) and Tridimas and Gari (2010).
4 This provision on free movement of capital dates back to the Maastricht Treaty.
5 Nyikos (2003) found, that over half of Court rulings lead to settlement by the parties without the need for further national court intervention.
6 Directive 77/388 on the harmonization of laws relating to turnover taxes, OJ 1997, L 145/1. For the list of amendments see http://europa.eu/legislation_summaries/other/l31006_en.htm#AMENDINGACT (accessed 1 April 2011).

REFERENCES

Alter, K.J. and Vargas, J. (2000) 'Explaining variation in the use of European litigation strategies: European Community law and gender equality policy', *Comparative Political Studies* 33(4): 452–82.

Alter, K.J. (2009) *The European Court's Political Power*, Oxford: Oxford University Press.
Andersen, M.S. and Liefferink, D. (eds) (1997) *European Environmental Policy: The Pioneers*, Manchester: Manchester University Press.
Barber, S.A. (2003) *Welfare and the Constitution*, Princeton, NJ: Princeton University Press.
Börzel, T. (2001) 'Non-compliance in the European Union: pathology or statistical artefact?' *Journal of European Public Policy* 8(5): 803–24.
Brunell, T.L., Stone Sweet, A. and Harlow, C. (2008) , 'Litigating the Treaty of Rome: the European Court of Justice and Articles 226, 230, and 234', *New Modes of Governance Project*, available at http://www.eu-newgov.org/datalists/deliverables_detail.asp?Project_ID=26 (accessed 7 September 2011).
Carrubba, C.J., Gabel, M. and Hankla, C. (2008) 'Judicial behavior under political constraints: evidence from the European Court of Justice', *American Political Science Review* 102(4): 435–52.
Chalmers, D. (2000) 'The positioning of EU judicial politics within the United Kingdom', *West European Politics* 23(4): 169–210.
Chalmers, D., Davies, G. and Monti, G. (2010) *European Union Law*, 2nd edn, Cambridge: Cambridge University Press.
Chaves, M. (2011) , 'European criminal law: reshaping criminal justice across the European Union?', Ph.D. dissertation, London School of Economics and Political Science.
Cichowski, R. (2007) *The European Court and Civil Society: Litigation, Mobilisation and Governance*, Cambridge: Cambridge University Press.
European Commission (2010) '27th annual report on the monitoring of the application of EU law', COM (2010) 538 final.
European Court of Justice (2008) *Annual Report of the European Court of Justice 2007*, Luxembourg.
European Court of Justice (2009) *Annual Report of the European Court of Justice 2008*, Luxembourg.
European Court of Justice (2010) *Annual Report of the European Court of Justice 2009*, Luxembourg.
Fligstein, N. (2008) *Euro-Clash: The EU, European Identity and the Future of Europe*, Oxford: Oxford University Press.
Fligstein, N. and McNichol, J. (1998) 'The institutional terrain of the European Union', in W. Sandholtz and A. Stone Sweet (eds), *European Integration and Supranational Governance*, Oxford: Oxford University Press, pp. 59–91.
Friedman, B. (2003) 'Mediated popular constitutionalism', *Michigan Law Review* 101(8): 2596–636.
Gibson, J.L., Caldeira, G.A. and Spence, L.K. (2005) 'Why do people accept public policies they oppose? Testing legitimacy theory with a survey-based experiment', *Political Research Quarterly* 58(2): 187–201.
Granger, M.-P. (2004) 'When governments go to Luxembourg . . . : the influence of governments on the European Court of Justice', *European Law Review* 29(1): 1–31.
Harding, C. and Gibbs, A. (2005) 'Why go to Court in Europe? An analysis of cartel appeals 1995–2004', *European Law Review* 30(3): 349–69.
Héritier, A., Knill, C. and Mingers, S. (1996) *Ringing the Changes in Europe: Regulatory Competition and the Transformation of the State. Britain, France, Germany*, Berlin: De Gruyter.
Howse, R.L. and Teitel, R. (2010) 'Beyond compliance: rethinking why international law really matters', *Global Policy* 1(2): 127–36.
Jupille, J. and Caporaso, J.A. (2009) 'Domesticating discourses: European law, English judges, and political institutions', *European Political Science Review* 1(2): 205–28.

Kelemen, R.D. (2011) *Eurolegalism: The Transformation of Law and Regulation in the European Union*, Cambridge: Harvard University Press.
Komárek, J. (2011) 'Precedent in European Union law: reasoning with previous decisions of the Court of Justice', Ph.D. dissertation, Faculty of Law, University of Oxford.
Maduro, M.P. (1998) *We the Court: The European Court of Justice and the European Economic Constitution*, Oxford and Portland, OR: Hart Publishing.
Miceli, T.J. and Coşgel, M.M. (1994) 'Reputation and judicial decision making', *Journal of Economic Behavior and Organisation* 23(1): 31–51.
Murphy, W.F. (2007) *Constitutional Democracy*, Baltimore, MD: Johns Hopkins University Press.
Nyikos, S.A. (2003) "The preliminary reference process: national court implementation, changing opportunity structures and litigant desistment", *European Union Politics* 4(4): 397–419.
Penner, J.E. (2003) 'Legal reasoning and the authority of law', in L.H. Meyer, S. Paulson and T. Pogge (eds), *Rights, Culture, and the Law: Themes from the Legal and Political Philosophy of Joseph Raz*, Oxford: Oxford University Press, pp. 71–97.
Rawlings, R. (1993) 'The Eurolaw game: some deductions from a saga', *Journal of Law and Society* 20(3): 309–40.
Rogers, J.R. (2001) 'Information and judicial review: a signalling game of legislative–judicial interaction', *American Journal of Political Science* 45(1): 84–99.
Schauer, F. (2000) 'Incentives, reputation and the inglorious determinants of judicial behaviour', *Cincinnati Law Review* 68(3): 615–36.
Schepel, H. and Wesseling, R. (1997) 'The legal community: judges, lawyers, officials and clerks in the writing of Europe', *European Law Journal* 3(2): 165–88.
Slagter, T.H. (2009) 'National parliaments and the ECJ: a view from the Bundestag', *Journal of Common Market Studies* 47(1): 175–97.
Stein, E. (1981) 'Lawyers, judges, and the making of a transnational constitution', *American Journal of International Law* 75(1): 1–27.
Stone Sweet, A. and Caporaso, J.A. (1998) 'From free trade to supranational polity: the European Court and integration', in W. Sandholtz and A. Stone Sweet (eds), *European Integration and Supranational Governance*, Oxford: Oxford University Press, pp. 92–133.
Terra, B.J.M. and Wattel, P. (2008) *European Tax Law*, Deventer: Kluwer.
Tridimas, T. and Gari, G. (2010) 'Winners and losers in Luxembourg: a statistical analysis of judicial review before the European Court of Justice and the Court of First Instance (2001–2005)', *European Law Review* 35(2): 131–73.
Vanberg, G. (2001) 'Legislative–judicial relations: a game-theoretic approach to constitutional review', *American Political Science Review* 45(2): 346–61.

The political foundations of judicial independence in the European Union

R. Daniel Kelemen

ABSTRACT This contribution explores the political foundations of judicial independence in the European Union and asks to what degree the ECJ is insulated against court curbing mechanisms that might threaten judicial independence. The contribution reviews the major court curbing mechanisms identified in the literature on American law and politics and assesses the extent to which these mechanisms might be applied in restraining the ECJ. The evidence and analysis suggests that the ECJ is remarkably well insulated against each of the major court curbing mechanisms identified in the literature.

INTRODUCTION

A rich literature documents that the European Court of Justice (ECJ)[1] has played a central role in driving forward the process of European integration (Alter 2001; Burley and Mattli 1993; Stein 1981; Stone Sweet 2004; Weiler 1991). The European Union's (EU) judicial system also plays a central role in the day-to-day governance of the EU (Stone Sweet 2010), as EU policy-makers rely heavily on the ECJ and national courts to make up for the EU's lack of a strong administrative apparatus (Kelemen 2011).

The ECJ is an essential 'engine' of European integration (Pollack 2003), but it is also an engine under strain. The ECJ faces a daunting set of challenges. The growing scope of EU law and the enlargement of the EU are bringing ever more cases to the ECJ's docket. As EU law expands into more sensitive areas of national policy, such as healthcare, education and taxation, the ECJ is pressed to step into terrain where its decisions are more likely to spark public outcries and political reprisals. The formal adoption of the Charter of Fundamental Rights in the Lisbon Treaty will open new fields of rights litigation, leading the ECJ into even more sensitive terrain.

Courts that overstep the boundaries that countervailing political powers or the public are willing to accept may face political backlash and be subject to a variety of 'court curbing' mechanisms. The likelihood of political actors or the public punishing or in some way restraining courts depends both on the institutional setting in which the courts are embedded and on prevailing norms regarding political interference with judiciary (Vanberg 2008). The literature on European legal integration has identified a number of the institutional features of the EU that insulate the ECJ from threats of legislative override and other forms of reprisal by member state governments. However, none of this literature provides a full account of the variety of court curbing mechanisms that political actors can employ and the extent to which the ECJ is insulated against them. This paper reviews the primary court curbing mechanisms identified in the literature on law and politics and explores the extent to which the ECJ is insulated against these mechanisms.

The analysis highlights the political foundations of the remarkable degree of independence that the ECJ enjoys. Not only does the EU's 'joint decision trap' (Scharpf 1988) insulate the ECJ against threats of legislative or constitutional override, as many have rightly argued (Pollack 2003; Stone Sweet 2000), the roots of the ECJ's independence are even deeper and more secure. I demonstrate that, contrary to claims made by Gibson and Caldeira (Caldeira and Gibson 1995, 1997; Gibson and Caldeira 1995, 1998), public opinion provides a solid base of 'diffuse support' for the court. Also, exploring the internal organization of the ECJ, I show why member states' ability to influence the court through appointments is limited.

The next section of the contribution reviews the major court curbing mechanisms identified in the literature on law and politics. The third section assesses the extent to which these mechanisms might be applied in restraining the ECJ and argues that the ECJ is remarkably well insulated against them. The fourth section concludes.

COURT CURBING MECHANISMS

The study of court curbing mechanisms – mechanisms through which political actors can influence courts to make judgments that do not diverge excessively from the political actors' preferences[2] – is well developed in the literature on American law and politics. Although the institutional context in which the ECJ operates of course differs from that in which the United States (US) Supreme Court operates, the mechanisms identified in the American politics literature are generic enough that one might expect variants of them to be found, or at least to be feasible, in any democratic polity – including the EU. These mechanisms include: (1) *legislative or constitutional override* – legislation or constitutional amendments that override court decisions (Epstein and Knight 1998; Eskridge 1991; Ferejohn and Shipan 1990); (2) *resource punishment* – withholding funding from the court system or tampering with judges' pay (Cross and Nelson 2001: 1465–9; Ferejohn 1998: 356); (3) *jurisdiction stripping* – removing particular areas of law from the court's jurisdiction (Chutkow 2008; Cross and Nelson 2001: 1463–4); (4) *court packing* – expanding the size of courts so as to stack them with judges that better reflect the preferences of political actors (Figueiredo and Tiller 1996; Gely and Spiller 1992); and (5) *judicial selection and reappointment* – using the power of appointment or reappointment of judges to staff the court with judges who reflect political actors' preferences (Shepherd 2009). Some studies focus on particular mechanisms, while others focus on identifying periods of court curbing in which a number of the mechanisms listed above may have been threatened or carried out (Clark 2009; Nagel 1965; Rosenberg 1992).

The literature on court curbing mechanisms in the US finds that proposals for court curbing measures are almost never enacted, and yet many scholars suggest that these mechanisms nevertheless do influence the Supreme Court (Clark 2009, 2011; Farganis 2009; Glick 2009; Handberg and Hill 1980; Whittington 2003).[3] Some would argue that this is a product of observational equivalence, in which the fact that court curbing proposals are not enacted should not be taken as evidence of their weakness, but rather as an indication that the threat posed by the mere discussion of such proposals is sufficient to rein in courts – making their enactment unnecessary. Clark's recent work (2009, 2011) offers a sophisticated analysis of why the US Supreme Court might be influenced by proposals for court curbing measures, even if there is very little chance these measures would actually be enacted. He argues that the mere introduction of court curbing bills in Congress serves as a signal to the Court that its public legitimacy is waning.

The notion that court curbing measures have an impact because they signal the erosion of the public legitimacy of the Court brings us to our sixth court curbing mechanism: *public opinion*. Public opinion is not a direct court curbing mechanism in the sense of the measures discussed above. Rather, public support for courts is a bulwark of judicial independence, and erosion of support weakens the court's defenses against potential attacks. According to Easton (1965: 273), every public institution needs a certain 'reservoir of favourable attitudes or good will' that makes members of the public willing to accept policy outputs to which they are opposed. For unelected supreme courts, this diffuse public support is a particularly crucial shield against political interference. The higher the levels of diffuse public support for a court, the greater the costs politicians will face for attempting to undermine that court's independence or to otherwise challenge its rulings (Caldeira 1987; Caldeira and Gibson 1992; McGuire and Stimson 2004). Given the importance of diffuse public support, courts must be careful to maintain their reservoir of public good will.

COURT CURBING IN THE EU . . . AND WHY IT DOES NOT WORK

An extensive literature on EU law and politics has established why it is so difficult for member states to rein in the ECJ by passing legislation or making treaty amendments to reverse its decisions or to otherwise attack the institutional foundations of the Court (see, for instance, Alter 2001; Pollack 2003; Stone Sweet 2000; Stone Sweet and Brunell 2011). In short, court curbing mechanisms – such as *legislative or constitutional/treaty override, resource punishment, jurisdiction stripping or court packing* – that would require the passage of treaty amendments or of EU legislation face a daunting set of challenges. Given the multiple veto players (Tsebelis 2002) in the EU political system, the diversity of member state preferences and the high threshold required for collective decisions, EU member states are unable to agree on measures needed to rein in or discipline the ECJ. They face what Scharpf (1988) has labeled a joint decision trap. Where amendments to the EU treaties are necessary to reverse an ECJ decision, member states must convene an intergovernmental conference, reach unanimous agreement on amendments and have the amended treaty ratified at the national level. The hurdles to legislative court curbing measures are also high. Most EU legislation is subject to the co-decision procedure (now referred to as the ordinary legislative procedure), in which the European Commission must initiate a legislative proposal and in which passage of legislation requires not only a qualified majority vote in the Council of Ministers, but also a majority vote in the European Parliament.

Attempting to curb ECJ activism through 'resource punishment' would be more problematic still, for two reasons. First, the European Parliament plays a powerful role in shaping the EU's budget; given that the Parliament is generally sympathetic to controversial ECJ rulings that extend the scope or depth of European integration, it would be likely to block any efforts to use the budget to punish the Court. Second, the pay of ECJ judges is governed by the same Staff Regulations that govern the pay of all EU officials; thus, judges cannot be singled out for financial punishment through their pay.

Jurisdiction stripping, which involves removing particular areas of law from the court's jurisdiction, requires treaty changes that necessitate unanimous agreement of the member states. Certainly, EU member states have attempted to act preemptively to keep particular areas of law out of the ECJ's jurisdiction. A central point of the 'pillar structure' put in place by the Maastricht Treaty was to ensure that policy areas such as immigration and asylum would not be subject to ECJ jurisdiction.[4] Likewise, protocols appended to EU treaties have sometimes aimed at limiting ECJ jurisdiction over particular issues for particular member states, as for instance with Protocol 30 to the Lisbon Treaty exempting the UK and Poland from the application of the Charter of Fundamental Rights. However, retroactive jurisdiction stripping – stripping of areas previously conferred to the ECJ or in which the Court had asserted jurisdiction – has never occurred in the EU.

Even if we accept that the actual adoption of court curbing measures would be exceedingly rare in the EU, the literature cited above reminds us that the discussion of such measures might send a signal to the court that its public legitimacy is waning and lead the court to exercise self-restraint. To assess this claim, we must turn to the literature on public opinion on the ECJ.

Diffuse public support

Very little research has been conducted on the impact of public opinion on the ECJ, or conversely on the impact of controversial ECJ rulings on public opinion concerning the Court. The most widely cited papers on this topic were published in the 1990s by Gibson and Caldeira (Caldeira and Gibson 1995, 1997; Gibson and Caldeira 1995, 1998). They started from the premise that maintaining diffuse public support was essential for the ECJ, particularly because, like other courts, it lacked, 'any electoral connection from which to draw legitimacy' and because 'it has taken such a forceful and increasingly prominent role in leading European integration' (Gibson and Caldeira 1998: 69–70).

Gibson and Caldeira's central claim was that the ECJ did not enjoy high levels of diffuse public support and that if the ECJ made unpopular decisions it would risk prompting a damaging political backlash. They concluded that, 'the Court rests on a precarious bedrock of support. To the extent it performs well, support will be forthcoming. To the extent it becomes enmeshed in controversial legal disputes, its support is certainly at risk' (Ibid: 90). Gibson and Caldeira did scholars a great service with their pioneering research on public support for the ECJ. However, subsequent developments in support for the ECJ have not borne out their hypotheses. The ECJ has continued to push forward the frontiers of integration and to make highly controversial rulings, but has not been subject to a damaging backlash or a decline in public support.

This paper challenges Gibson and Caldeira's analysis and explains why the ECJ has fared so much better than they expected. Gibson and Caldeira attempted to gauge levels of diffuse public support for the ECJ in absolute terms, according to a scale they developed for the purpose of assessing the legitimacy of the ECJ. I suggest a different approach: levels of diffuse public support can only be gauged in relative terms. In an environment where public institutions are widely despised, those that are even moderately respected may be in a position of strength relative to other political institutions that might attack them.

That is precisely the circumstance in which the ECJ operates. While citizens do not hold the ECJ in an exalted position, it is easily the most trusted institution of government in Europe at the EU or national level. Consider Figures 1 and 2. Figure 1, drawn from Eurobarometer surveys conducted between 1999 and 2010,[5] shows that far more EU citizens trust the ECJ than distrust it. Moreover, levels of trust in the ECJ and 'net trust' in the ECJ (the percent who trust the Court minus the percent who distrust it) have both increased during this period. These trends clearly contradict Gibson and Caldeira's (1998) expectations, as they expressed concern (writing in the mid-1990s) that the Court's weak and unstable levels of diffuse public support might deteriorate in coming years.

But Figure 1 treats the ECJ in isolation and the levels of diffuse support it suggests are not particularly impressive considered on their own. Figure 2 assesses net trust in the ECJ relative to net trust in other governmental institutions. Here the data is more striking. The ECJ is consistently and by far the most trusted governmental institution in Europe. It is also the only one that consistently has positive net trust scores.

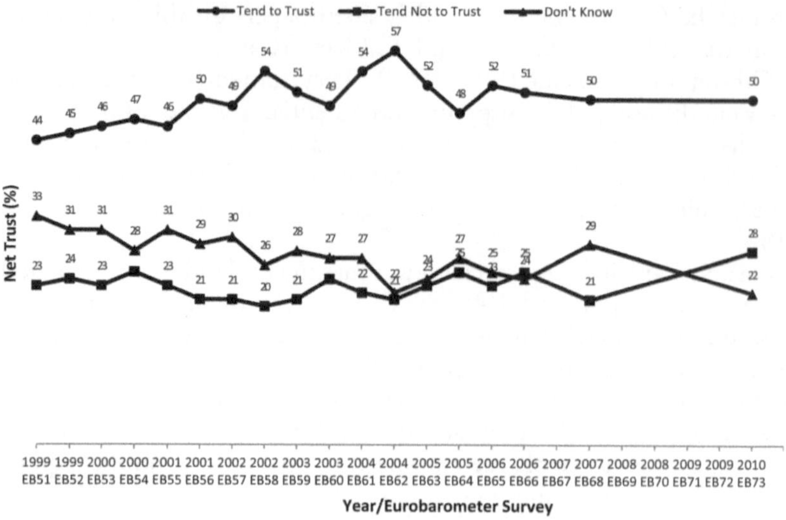

Figure 1 Trust in the European Court of Justice – % EU

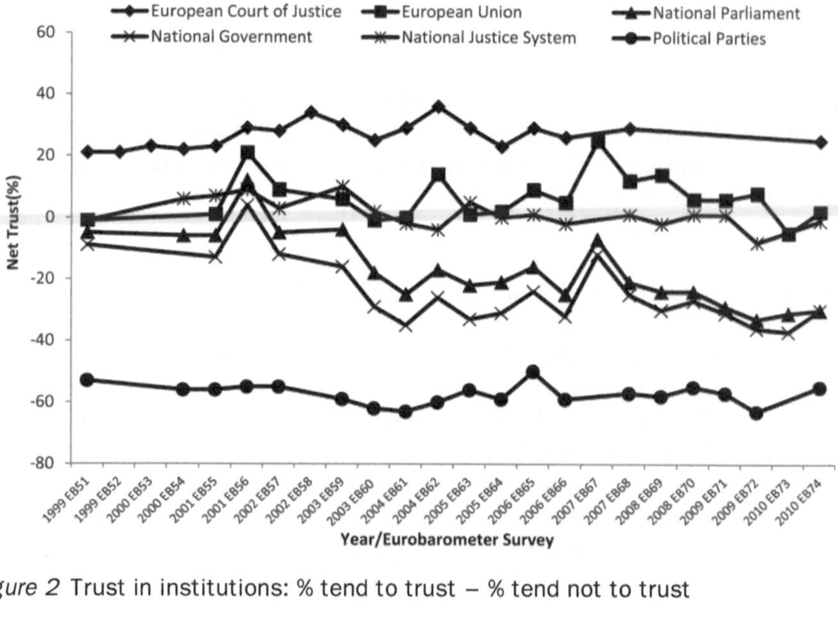

Figure 2 Trust in institutions: % tend to trust – % tend not to trust

Why are the data in Figure 2 significant? The data speak directly to the question of whether the ECJ has grounds to fear criticism or threats of various curbing measures made by national politicians. As discussed above, we know that the likelihood that court curbing measures could be introduced is very low owing to the joint decision trap. But in principle the possibility remains that the mere voicing of criticism or of threats – even threats that would never be carried out – may harm a court by undermining public support for it (Clark 2011). In the ECJ's case, this seems highly unlikely. The politicians leveling those threats, and the parliaments and governments in which they are represented, are held in such low regard that the ECJ might well welcome their attacks. Given the unpopularity of national political parties, being attacked by national politicians may in fact be a boon to the ECJ. The ECJ might actually curry favor with the public by battling with national politicians. Moreover, being criticized by member states and not bowing to them may also signal the ECJ's strength.[6]

Finally, because data on average levels of trust may mask variation between member states, it is worthwhile to consider trends at the national level. In particular, one might expect that highly controversial and highly publicized ECJ decisions that were widely seen as going against the interests of a particular member state might lead to decreases in public levels of trust in the Court in that state. To explore that hypothesis, let us consider shifts in public trust of the ECJ in the six countries that were directly involved in three cases that were easily the most controversial and highly publicized ECJ decisions in recent years, *Laval* (C-341/05), *Viking* (C-438/05) and *Rüffert* (C-346/06). These three cases, which each involved issues concerning the freedom to provide services in the EU, were widely seen as undermining systems of collective bargaining in West European social democracies and more generally as threatening to encourage a race to the bottom in wages and working conditions. Although all three cases involved private economic actors, each essentially pitted the interests of a new member state from Eastern Europe against a higher wage member state from Western Europe. *Viking* pitted Estonia against Finland, *Laval* Latvia against Sweden and *Rüffert* Poland against Germany. Finland, Sweden and Germany were seen as the 'losers' in these cases; Estonia, Latvia and Poland as the 'winners'. In each case, there was widespread denunciation of the rulings by prominent political actors, in particular those associated with the labor unions and left parties, in the 'losing' states (see Blauberger [2012] for a discussion of political reactions to the cases).

What impact did these rulings and the political reactions to them have on public support for the ECJ? Consider the data in Figure 3. The ECJ ruled on *Viking* and *Laval* in December 2007 and on *Rüffert* in April 2008. Yet, between 2008 and 2010, public trust in the ECJ in Finland and Sweden, two of the countries who were ostensibly aggrieved by the rulings, increased substantially. In Sweden, trust in the ECJ reached an all time high. Only in Germany did net trust in the ECJ decrease, and even there it simply returned to a level that was well within the norm of its historical levels of net support for the Court.

In short, average levels of public trust in the ECJ across Europe are far higher than levels of trust in other governmental institutions, they are relatively stable over the last decade and evidence does not seem to suggest that they decrease in response to controversial Court rulings.

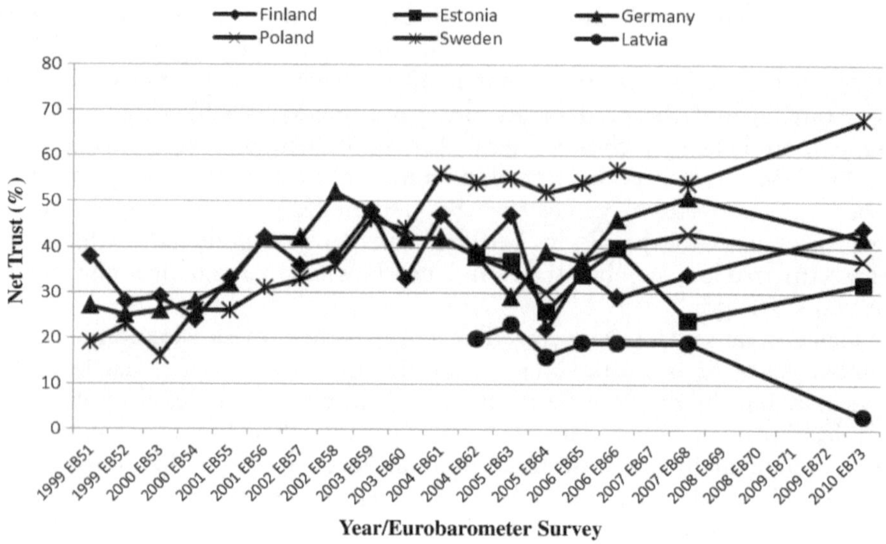

Figure 3 Trust in the European Court of Justice (% trust – % not trust)

Judicial selection and retention

If member state governments cannot credibly threaten to adopt court curbing measures or to erode public support for the Court by denouncing its rulings, they may seek to rein in the court through their power of appointment. Without question, the power of appointment is a vital means through which democratically elected branches of government shape the EU judicial system over time. ECJ judges are appointed for six-year renewable terms. The judges' decisions are shielded from scrutiny by their governments through the Court's practice of issuing decisions as the consensus of the Court and not publishing dissenting opinions. Nevertheless, certainly it is possible that governments would seek to appoint judges that shared their ideological orientation or more specifically their position with regard to the preferred pace and depth of European integration. They could do this through their routine processes of appointment and reappointment of judges, or – at least in principle – if faced with a Court that was acting in ways they could not tolerate, they might attempt to quickly 'pack' the Court by enlarging the number of judges and putting in place new judges that would tip the balance on the Court toward politically acceptable positions.[7]

Given the enormous volume of literature on the ECJ, there is shockingly little written on the process through which ECJ justices are appointed. The most extensive article was written by Kenney in 1998. Her account highlighted some of the procedures through which national governments chose their justices and the backgrounds of the judges various member states tended to select. Likewise Cohen's (2008) historical account looks at the professional backgrounds of ECJ judges, focusing on the shift toward selection of more justices with academic backgrounds. As to whether the selection and re-appointment (or replacement) of justices is politicized in an effort to limit judicial activism on the Court, we know very little. Alter's (1998: 139) research found that of the many factors that went into deciding national appointments to the ECJ, efforts to limit judicial activism on the court were only a factor in Germany and France.

Our understanding of the EU judicial system could benefit greatly from in-depth empirical research on the politics of appointments to the ECJ. This contribution's ambitions are more modest and it does not provide new evidence in that regard. What it does instead is to offer an analysis designed to demonstrate the limits of judicial appointments as a mechanism to 'rein in' the ECJ. Certainly, if all member state governments suddenly agreed that the ECJ had gone too far in advancing European integration and each, at the next opportunity, replaced their national judge with a fervent Euroskeptic, then over the course of a few years the Court's approach would likely change and it would no longer act as the aggressive engine of integration that it so long has. But that scenario is fanciful. The more realistic scenario we should consider is whether one, or a handful, of Euroskeptic governments could influence the direction of ECJ jurisprudence by appointing new Euroskeptic judges, or perhaps by somehow influencing their existing judges to adjust their positions to accord with the increasingly Euroskeptic views of their home country.[8] And as we shall see, the impact of the appointment of one or even a handful of such judges on ECJ doctrine is likely to be minimal.

To understand the likely impact of the appointments, we must first understand how the Court organizes its work. Malecki (2012) has shed light on a vital aspect of the ECJ's organization by highlighting the growing role of the system of chambers. While the ECJ announces its decisions as rulings of 'the Court', in fact the full Court of 27 judges almost never hears a case as a group and has not done so at all in the past two years. Instead, the Court divides itself into a number of chambers that actually hear cases in the name of the Court. The most significant cases are heard by the 'Grand Chamber' composed of 13 judges. Most other cases are heard by chambers composed of five judges. The most routine cases are heard by chambers of three judges. The judges seek to build consensus, but where necessary they take a majority vote and the minority justices thereafter remain silent – not issuing dissenting opinions.

The procedure through which chambers are formed operates as follows.[9] Every three years, following the partial replacement of ECJ judges provided for in the Treaties, the judges elect a President from amongst themselves. They also elect the Presidents of the eight chambers of the Court.[10] The President of the ECJ then appoints the remaining judges to the chambers. Given that cases are heard by subsets of judges, it is of course possible that different chambers – reflecting the preferences of their judges – would interpret EU law differently from one another (see Malecki 2012). Such discrepancies would represent a threat to legal consistency at the apex of the EU judicial system. Moreover, the possibility that small subsets of judges could shape

ECJ doctrine could offer an opportunity for individual member states to use their power of appointment to decisively influence the development of European law. Does the chamber system represent a threat to legal consistency and an opportunity for judges with 'extreme' views (i.e., ones that might be appointed by Euroskeptic governments to rein in judicial activism on the court) to shape doctrine? It seems not.

The ECJ organizes its work in a way that minimizes the potential influence of judges who are preference outliers. Generally, the more significant the case, the more judges that sit on the chamber that hears the case (i.e., the most routine cases are heard by chambers of three, more significant cases by chambers of five and the most significant cases by the Grand Chamber of 13). This hierarchy assures that more significant cases will be heard by groups of judges in which the median judge (who casts the deciding vote) is more likely to be positioned close to the median judge of the full Court of 27. In other words, if a member state appointed a Euroskeptic judge to the ECJ with an eye toward reining in judicial activism, that judge would likely never find herself in the position to determine the outcome of the case as the median justice on a panel. Instead, when hearing important cases that judge would find herself sitting with a group of judges that would effectively cancel out her views. In this respect, the ECJ organizes its work in a manner that parallels that found in many judicial systems – in which a judicial hierarchy of increasingly large, collegial courts serves to structurally constrain the ability of any individual judge to make 'aberrant' decisions (Ferejohn and Kramer 2002; Kornhauser and Sager 1986). Moreover, it also seems plausible that the President of the Court might appoint judges to chambers strategically – so as to put together chambers that reflect a balance of attitudes toward European integration and that minimize the impact of outliers.[11]

To further explore whether the chamber system represents a threat to legal consistency within the court and an opportunity for Euroskeptic judges to rein in pro-integration judicial activism, we can conduct a brief theoretical exercise. Simply for the purposes of this exercise, let us assume that each judge's position on the appropriate depth of European integration reflects the level of public support for European integration in their member state. The level of public support can be expected to shape governments' positions on European integration, at least over the long term, and therefore to influence the types of judges that governments might appoint.[12] Moreover, if sitting judges are concerned about the degree of support for deeper European integration of their government and their home country's population, they might be influenced by the public attitudes reflected in these opinion surveys. Figure 4 presents 'net support for integration' scores for each member state based on Eurobarometer data.[13] This data provide us with a measure of the degree of public support for European integration across countries.

Based on these data, we can rank judges on a 'European integration scale' in which judges from states with low levels of net public support for European integration are presumed to be more Euroskeptic and judges from states with higher levels of public support for integration are presumed to be more

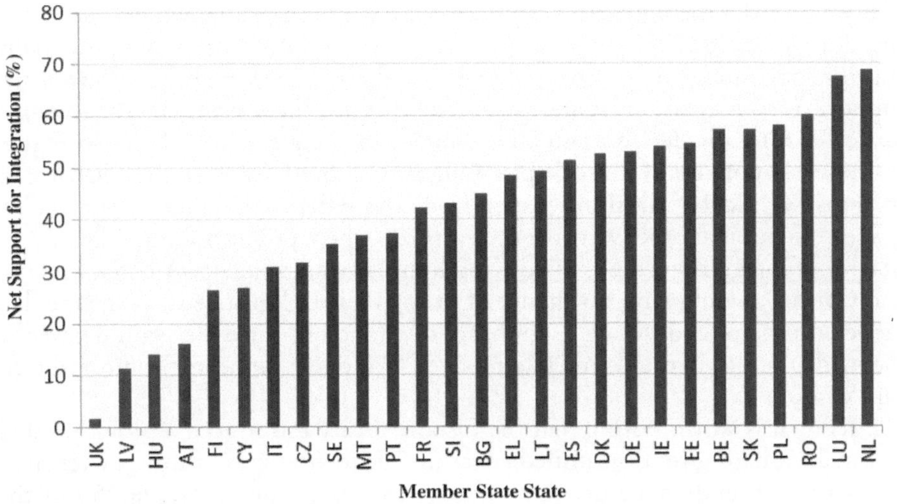

Figure 4 Average support for integration, 2007–2010

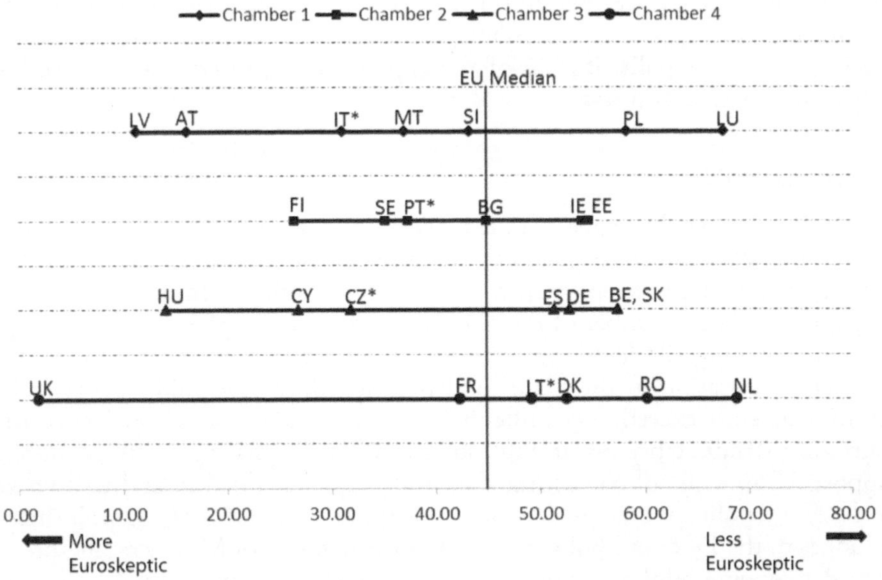

Figure 5 Judge positions by chamber
Note: * Most Euroskeptic median judge.

supportive of integration. Figure 5 shows us the composition of each chamber in today's ECJ and helps us to consider the likelihood that a Euroskeptic judge would be able to influence its rulings.

If we consider the potential combinations of five judges that would hear cases, the third judge from the left in each chamber would be the most potentially 'Euroskeptic' judge (i.e., the judge from the country with the lowest net support for integration score) who could find themselves as the median justice, casting the decisive vote in a chamber hearing a case.[14] Thus, in Figure 5, the most potentially Euroskeptic judge who could serve as a median judge in a case would be the third justice from the left in Chamber 1 (the Italian judge). To put it another way, the six countries where public opinion is least supportive of integration (the United Kingdom, Latvia, Hungary, Austria, Finland and Cyprus), would have no chance of seeing their ECJ justice sit as the median judge on a chamber deciding a significant case (and of course they would never be the median judge in the Grand Chamber of 13 judges that hears the most significant cases).

Finally, it is worth noting that the Lisbon Treaty introduced a provision that will make it harder for disgruntled governments to attempt to throw a wrench in the works by sending a Euroskeptic judge to Luxembourg. Article 255 of the Treaty establishes an appointment panel that screens and gives opinions on candidates' 'suitability to perform the duties of Judge and Advocate General of the Court of Justice and General Court before the governments of the member states make the appointments'. Thus far, the panel's activities are shrouded in secrecy, but it was established as a way of providing an additional check on excessive politicization of the appointment process and of ensuring independence of ECJ justices.

CONCLUSION

The ECJ's remarkable degree of independence has strong political foundations. The ECJ is well insulated against the range of court curbing mechanisms that political actors have been known to deploy in other democratic polities. Together, the large number of member states, the high degree of political fragmentation among EU legislative actors, the judicial appointment process, the internal organization of the Court and the high degree of public support for the ECJ make it exceedingly difficult for political actors to directly curb the court or to indirectly cow it into submission by signaling shifts in public support. Ultimately, of course, the ECJ is deeply embedded in and responsive to the EU's political system. Member governments control the appointment of judges to the ECJ, and political actors in the Council of Ministers, the European Parliament and the Commission shape the legal norms that the ECJ must interpret and enforce. But within this very broad set of political constraints, the ECJ enjoys a remarkable degree of independence.

Biographical note: R. Daniel Kelemen is Jean Monnet Chair, Associate Professor of Political Science and Director of the Center for European Studies at Rutgers University.

ACKNOWLEDGEMENTS

I thank Terence Teo and Joshua Eaise for their research assistance and thank Philipp Genschel, Fritz Scharpf, Diana Panke, Maurits van der Veen, participants in the University of Bremen workshop, and three anonymous reviewers for their comments.

NOTES

1 With the Lisbon Treaty, the ECJ's official name became 'the Court of Justice'. Collectively, the Court of Justice, the General Court (formerly the Court of First Instance) and the Civil Service Tribunal constitute 'the Court of Justice of the European Union'.

2 While many scholars focus specifically on court curbing mechanisms imposed through legislation, I employ an expansive definition of court curbing mechanisms that allows us to include political control over appointments and the influence of public opinion as discussed below.

3 While Farganis (2009) speaks of a growing consensus that fears of court curbing influence justices, some leading scholars argue that threats of court curbing measures have little impact on the court. See, for instance, Baum (2003).

4 With the adoption of the Lisbon Treaty (and with it the repeal of Articles 35 EU and 68 EC), the pillar structure was eliminated and the ECJ gained general jurisdiction over the fields of freedom, security and justice. However, the ECJ's jurisdiction with respect to Common Foreign and Security Policy remains limited.

5 This article draws on data gathered from the European Commission's semi-annual Eurobarometer public opinion surveys carried out from 1999–2010 (Eurobarometer 51–74), a total of 24 surveys, which are available at http://ec.europa.eu/public_opinion/archives/eb_arch_en.htm (last accessed 1 July 2011).

6 In the US context, Lasser (1988) argues that unsuccessful attacks on the Supreme Court may signal to the public the Court's strength.

7 In practice, such rapid court packing would be implausible in the EU, given the great diversity of member state preferences and their commitment to defending the norm that each state can appoint one judge to the Court. The only circumstance in which one can imagine a rapid enlargement of the European judiciary would involve the creation of new courts alongside the ECJ, as for instance occurred with the creation of the Court of First Instance.

8 There is no clear causal mechanism through which governments could exercise this influence on sitting justices short of direct – and entirely illicit – contacts.

9 This description of the procedures follows from the rules presented in the Consolidated Version of the Rules of Procedure of the Court of Justice (OJ C 177/01, 2 July 2010) and in the Protocol (No 3) on the Statute of the Court of Justice of the European Union (OJ C 115/210, 9 May 2008), supplemented by personal communication with Miguel Maduro, former Advocate General on the Court.

10 The top vote-getters become Presidents of the first four chambers. These chambers, which are composed of six or seven judges, hear cases in groups of five. Chambers number five through eight are composed of the exact same judges as chambers one through four, except that the Presidents of chambers one through four do not sit on

chambers five through eight. Chambers five through eight hear the most routine cases to come before the ECJ, and they hear them in groups of three judges.

11 Because the process through which the President of the Court assigns judges to chambers is secret and because the sample size is too small to enable us to detect a statistically significant deviation from a random selection process, we are unable to draw firm conclusions about the assignment process.

12 Given divisions between mass publics and élites over European integration, these scores of course do not perfectly reflect the support for integration among member state governments. An alternative approach would be to measure national governments support for European integration based on party manifesto data as Benoit and Laver (2006) and Voeten (2007) do or based on expert surveys that rate party positions on European integration as Marks *et al.* (2006) do. However, party manifesto and expert survey based datasets do not cover all 27 member states and are time constrained to particular years, whereas Eurobarometer surveys cover all member states and are repeated every six months.

13 These net scores represent the percentage of respondents who said their country's membership in the EU was a good thing, minus the percent who said it was a bad thing. The scores in Figure 4 are based on the average net score in each Eurobarometer survey conducted between 2007 and 2010 (Eurobarometers 67 through 72), the period since the EU reached its current size of 27 member states.

14 I do not consider chambers of three, because as noted above, they mostly hear routine cases. Of course, all things being equal, the likelihood that the median judge would hold a position that diverges significantly from the Court's median position is greater on a panel of three judges than on a panel of five.

REFERENCES

Alter, K. (1998) 'Who are the 'Masters of the Treaty'?: European governments and the European Court of Justice", *International Organization* 52(1): 121–47.

Alter, K. (2001) *Establishing the Supremacy of European Law*, Oxford: Oxford University Press.

Baum, L. (2003) 'The Supreme Court in American politics', *Annual Review of Political Science* 6: 161–80.

Benoit, K. and Laver, M. (2006) *Party Policy in Modern Democracies*, London: Routledge Press.

Blauberger, M. (2012) 'With Luxembourg in mind', *Journal of European Public Policy* 19(1): 109–26.

Burley, A.M. and Mattli, W. (1993) 'Europe before the court', *International Organization* 47(1): 41–76.

Caldeira, G.A. (1987) 'Public opinion and the US Supreme Court', *American Political Science Review* 81(4): 1139–53.

Caldeira, G.A. and Gibson, J.L. (1992) 'The etiology of public support for the Supreme Court', *American Journal of Political Science* 36(3): 635–64.

Caldeira, G.A. and Gibson, J.L. (1995) 'The legitimacy of the Court of Justice in the European Union', *The American Political Science Review* 89(2): 356–76.

Caldeira, G.A. and Gibson, J.L. (1997) 'Democracy and legitimacy in the European Union ", *International Social Science Journal* 49(2): 209–24.

Chutkow, D. (2008) 'Jurisdiction stripping', *Journal of Politics* 70(4): 1053–64.

Clark, T. (2009) 'The separation of powers, court curbing, and judicial legitimacy', *American Journal of Political Science* 53(4): 971–89.

Clark, T. (2011) *The Limits of Judicial Independence*, New York: Cambridge University Press.

Cohen, A. (2008) 'Scarlet robes, dark suits', *EUI Working Papers, RSCAS 2008/35*, RSCAS/EUI, Florence.
Cross, F. and Nelson, B. (2001) 'Strategic institutional effects on Supreme Court decisionmaking', *Northwestern University Law Review* 95(4): 1437–94.
Easton, D. (1965) *A Systems Analysis of Political Life*, New York: John Wiley and Sons.
Epstein, L. and Knight, J. (1998) *The Choices Justices Make*, Washington, DC: Congressional Quarterly Press.
Eskridge, W. (1991) 'Overriding Supreme Court statutory interpretation decisions', *The Yale Law Journal* 101(2): 331–455.
Farganis, D. (2009) 'Court curbing in the modern era: should Supreme Court Justices really worry about attacks from Congress?', available at http://ssrn.com/ (accessed 3 September 2010).
Ferejohn, J. (1998) 'Independent judges, dependent judiciary: explaining judicial independence', *Southern California Law Review* 72: 353–84.
Ferejohn, J. and Kramer, L. (2002) 'Independent judges, dependent judiciary: institutionalizing judicial restraint', *NYU Law Review* 77(4): 962–1039.
Ferejohn, J. and Shipan, C. (1990) 'Congressional influence on bureaucracy', *Journal of Law, Economics, & Organization* 6: 1–20.
Figueiredo, J. and Tiller, E. (1996) 'Congressional control of the courts', *Journal of Law and Economics* 39(2): 435–61.
Gely, R. and Spiller, P. (1992) 'The political economy of Supreme Court constitutional decisions', *International Review of Law and Economics* 12(1): 45–67.
Gibson, J.L. and Caldeira, G.A. (1995) 'The legitimacy of transnational legal institutions', *American Journal of Political Science* 39(2): 459–89.
Gibson, J.L. and Caldeira, G.A. (1998) 'Changes in the legitimacy of the European Court of Justice', *British Journal of Political Science* 28(1): 63–91.
Glick, D. (2009) 'Conditional strategic retreat', *The Journal of Politics* 71(3): 800–16.
Handberg, R. and Hill, H. (1980) 'Court curbing, court reversals, and judicial review', *Law & Society Review* 14(2): 309–22.
Kelemen, R.D. (2011) *Eurolegalism: The Transformation of Law and Regulation in the European Union*, Cambridge, MA: Harvard University Press.
Kenney, S. (1998) 'The members of the Court of Justice of the European Communities', *Columbia Journal of European Law* 5(1): 101–33.
Kornhauser, L. and Sager, L. (1986) 'Unpacking the court', *Yale Law Journal* 96: 115–17.
Lasser, W. (1988) *The Limits of Judicial Power*, Chapel Hill, NC: University of North Carolina Press.
Malecki, M. (2012) 'Do ECJ judges all speak with the same voice?', *Journal of European Public Policy* 19(1): 59–75.
Marks, G., Hooghe, L., Nelson, M. and Edwards, E. (2006) 'Party competition and European integration in the East and West', *Comparative Political Studies* 39(2): 155–75.
McGuire, K. and Stimson, K. (2004) 'The least dangerous branch revisited', *Journal of Politics* 66(4): 1018–35.
Nagel, S. (1965) 'Court-curbing periods in American history', *Vanderbilt Law Review* 18(3): 925–44.
Pollack, M. (2003) *The Engines of Integration*, Oxford: Oxford University Press.
Rosenberg, G. (1992) 'Judicial independence and the reality of political power', *The Review of Politics* 54(3): 369–98.
Scharpf, F. (1988) 'The joint-decision trap: lessons from German federalism and European integration', *Public Administration* 66(3): 239–78.
Shepherd, J. (2009) 'The influence of retention politics on judges' voting', *Journal of Legal Studies* 38(1): 169–203.

Stein, E. (1981) 'Lawyers, judges, and the making of a transnational constitution', *American Journal of International Law* 75(1): 1–27.
Stone Sweet, A. (2000) *Governing with Judges*, Oxford: Oxford University Press.
Stone Sweet, A. (2004) *The Judicial Construction of Europe*, Oxford: Oxford University Press.
Stone Sweet, A. (2010) 'The European Court of Justice and the judicialization of EU governance', *Living Reviews in European Governance* 5(2), available at http://europeangovernance.livingreviews.org/Articles/lreg-2010-2/ (accessed 8 September 2011).
Stone Sweet, A. and Brunell, T. (2011) 'How the European legal system works – and does not work', available at http://papers.ssrn.com/sol3/papers.cfm?abstract_id=1780902 (accessed 8 September 2011).
Tsebelis, G. (2002) *Veto Players*, Princeton, NJ: Princeton University Press.
Vanberg, G. (2008) 'Establishing and maintaining judicial independence', in K. Whittington, R.D. Kelemen and G. Caldeira (eds), *The Oxford Handbook of Law and Politics*, Oxford: Oxford University Press, pp. 99–118.
Voeten, E. (2007) 'The politics of international judicial appointments', *International Organization* 61(4): 669–701.
Weiler, J.H.H. (1991) 'The transformation of Europe', *Yale Law Journal* 100(8): 2403–83.
Whittington, K. (2003) 'Legislative sanctions and the strategic environment of judicial review', *I-Con: The International Journal of Constitutional Law* 1(3): 446–74.

Do ECJ judges all speak with the same voice? Evidence of divergent preferences from the judgments of chambers

Michael Malecki

ABSTRACT A considerable body of scholarly work has asserted that the ECJ's institutional independence has implied behavioural independence: in short, that the ECJ has pursued a pro-integration agenda perhaps at odds with national governments' preferences. But, inside the black box of the court's collective decisions, do judges share a common preference for expanding the authority of the Court and EU generally? While individual behaviour is not directly observable, the ECJ's system of chambers provides a potentially valuable window on the impact of individual decisions by subsets of the judges. I develop a statistical model, extending the item-response model to account for selective participation in decisions, to find evidence of individual behaviour in the collective judgments. Results for ECJ cases show that judges do not share uniform preferences, suggesting that institutional independence has provided cover for the court, and that judges' preferences lie on a continuum from Europhilia to Euroscepticism.

INTRODUCTION

The development of European Union (EU) law, and role of the European Court of Justice (ECJ) in that process, have attracted considerable scholarly attention, far beyond the present collection. In particular, scholars have examined how the ECJ, through interaction with national courts and private litigants, has established a supranational legal order that arguably exceeds what the member states of the EU desired (e.g., Alter 2001; Bobek 2008; Börzel 2003; Börzel *et al.* 2009; Garrett 1995; Héritier 2001; Mattli and Slaughter 1995, 1998 Stone Sweet and Brunell 1998). The general focus of this research was how the ECJ, pursuing a pro-integration agenda, was able to develop a legal system whereby its legal interpretations of the Treaties and the legislation of the EU gained the force of law in national legal systems.

The claim that ECJ judges behave together as a well-tuned 'engine of integration' has two parts, which have heretofore been untestable: (1) that ECJ judges' preferences are uniform; and (2) that judges' preferences are uniformly more in favour of European integration than those of member state governments. This contribution addresses the first part of that claim, finding evidence that outcomes vary systematically with the composition of chambers; that is, to the individual judges hearing a case. Evidence about the relationship between judges and their countries of origin is more tenuous, and I find a weak relationship with the left–right composition of appointing governments.

The *en banc* decisions of the court have prevented any individual-level analysis of decisions, and judges have remained 'mum' about the specifics of voting or any ideological differences among their ranks. In this contribution, I make use of a feature of the court's organization – the system of chambers – to investigate whether judges really are individually indistinguisable, as they are assumed to be in any case-level analysis. By constraining each decision to only the signatory judges, the model demonstrates evidence of a latent dimension of pro- or anti-Commission orientation. Cases are located with respect to the same dimension by the observations of member state governments relative to the Commission. Where other case-level analyses have found evidence of responsiveness to the Commission under various circumstances (Cichowski 1998, 2001, 2004; Slaughter *et al.* 1998; Stone Sweet and Brunell 1998) and to certain groupings of member states' observations (Carrubba *et al.* 2008), I investigate whether the Court's relationship with the Commission in particular is as singular as case-level analyses would have it.

Overall, it is impossible to deny that the ECJ as a whole shows evidence of pro-Commission leanings (which I call pro-integration). In the data at hand, the most 'anti-Commission' judge signed his name to pro-Commission judgments 72per cent of the time. Nevertheless, our understanding of judicial behaviour is enriched by considering the motivations and potential influences on individual judges rather than on the institution as a whole.

The ECJ enjoys considerable institutional insulation or *cover* under which it might advance some agenda. Judges are shielded from individual scrutiny by fixed renewable terms of office (not subject to recall), and their decisions are all ostensibly unanimous. No dissenting opinions about particular cases have ever been revealed, either in extended reasoning or simple individual voting details. The Court is clear that disagreements do arise in the secret deliberations, and that final decisions are made by majority rule. Given that decisions are made by chambers of as few as three judges, it could indeed be misleading to attribute to all judges and all groupings an identical motive.

The institutional insulation of the court does not imply a motive for individual judicial rulings. It simply provides cover, under which may lie a range of attitudes about integration, regulation and the appropriate level of government for regulation. Recognizing this, we must ask what motivates judges: the most common claim is that that they seek greater powers for the supranational institutions (Hartley 2007; Rasmussen 1986, 1998; Weiler 1994) or at least a particular view of supranational law common to all of them (Cichowski 2007; Héritier 2001; Wiklund 2003). Hartley puts it succinctly:

> One of the distinctive characteristics of the European Court is the extent to which its decision-making is based on policy. By policy is meant the values and attitudes of the judges – the objectives they wish to promote. The policies of the European Court are basically the following: 1) strengthening the Community (and especially the federal elements in it); 2) increasing the scope and effectiveness of Community law; 3) enlarging the powers of Community law. They may be summed up in one phrase: the promotion of European integration. (Hartley 2007: 76)

If we believe that disagreements do occur between judges voting on a case, then we must confront the fact that judges bring to bear their individual motivations when deciding cases. Although surely they share a common respect for the law, they must differ along a number of other dimensions that give rise to differences in their reasoned interpretations. Given the Court's diverse sources of appointment, it is at least plausible to expect member states in the aggregate to select judges that have heterogeneous preferences, reflecting to some degree the preferences of the several member state governments. This contribution finds clear evidence of systematic variation in outcomes that can be attributed to chamber composition, thus to individual judges; and suggestive evidence of a relationship with the governments that appoint them.

SOURCES AND CONSEQUENCES OF HETEROGENEOUS JUDICIAL MOTIVATIONS

Preliminary rulings make up the majority of the ECJ's work. They have served as the basis for many if not most of the ECJ's landmark decisions that have increased its own power and furthered integration. Moreover, they provide a source of cases – opportunity – for the Court irrespective of either the member state governments or of the Commission. Unlike actions for annulment or infringement proceedings, the rate of preliminary references is not subject to political control.

Observations, which announce the positions of the Commission and interested member states, are crucial components of the procedure at the Court of Justice and to our understanding of the Court's behaviour. The Commission makes observations in almost all preliminary reference cases, having a full-time Legal Service to monitor, prepare and argue cases before the ECJ. The observations in a case are confidential between the parties in the case and the Court, with no national government willing to make its written arguments public, and the Commission claiming its own right to secrecy under the Privacy Directive (95/46/EC).[1] According to the Commission Legal Service,[2] it 'routinely' intervenes in preliminary observations; it is generally accepted and expected that the Commission Legal Service will present the EU position on any matter before the Court.

The resources of the member states vary, as does the frequency with which they submit observations. The United Kingdom is, based on the author's search, the only one to provide citizens the means to request the submission of an observation.[3] Granger (2006: 35) calls intervention in ECJ cases a 'tool for influence' that governments were slow to exploit. In recent years patterns in observation-making behaviour are still inconsistent and vary as much with governments as with issue areas, though some are evident, for example, that 'Scandinavian countries and Austria tend to be very active in environmental matters' and 'the southern countries, such as Greece, Portugal, Spain and Italy, as well as France, put a great focus on agricultural issues' (Granger 2006: 38). Stein (1981) highlights their failure to make observations in early seminal preliminary-reference cases.

Some evidence supports the claim that the ECJ has navigated carefully the demands of member states. The empirical fact that member states comply with ECJ judgments, and that the ECJ has made some daring judgments and earned compliance, variously measured, despite some member state governments' grousing, does not establish independent unwanted action on the part of the Court.

It is more than plausible that the ECJ's decisions actually reflect the opinion of a majority of judges and, by imperfect proxy, a majority of member state governments that appointed them. Thus, an alternative claim is that the Court is acting within its discretion and has not been curtailed because the preferences of the judges are not at odds with those of the member states.

Many judges have served national-level non-judicial (appointive) posts, where they could demonstrate their fealty to national interest. But ECJ judges' terms are staggered, and elections are not at regular intervals, so a government does not know if it is going to be able to appoint a judge. A newly elected government may have to appoint a judge early in its term, which may in fact drive reappointment when governments do not invest in evaluating the sitting judge's behaviour compared to their preferences.

The appointment process, and the pool of potential appointees, varies considerably among the member states. It has also changed over time within member states. Two features of the methods of appointment to the ECJ suggest potential differences in the goals, preferences and motivations of judges. The first is of course cross-national variation resulting from different approaches to appointment and renewal or non-renewal. The second is, particularly for those countries that are more likely to make new appointments after each six-year term, that variations in the ideologies of national governments would affect the types of judges they select.

It is therefore plausible that governments would seek to appoint judges that share their preferences about the appropriate amount of government involvement in economic and social matters, or the appropriate level of government (national or European) to address those questions. It follows that one should expect judges of the Court of Justice to have a diversity of opinion.

Empirical opportunity: the system of chambers

The actual practice of the Court of Justice provides a rare opportunity to test whether its judges in fact have interchangeable preferences. The system of chambers, described below, reveals patterns in decision-making that vary not only with known features of cases but with the composition of the chamber hearing the case. To date, all analyses of the court have had to assume that all judges hold uniform preferences (generally assumed to be pro-integration), and that they all respond to signals and incentives uniformly. The variation in chambers may make it problematic to use the Court median as a measure of the ECJ's preferences, because each chamber median must be considered. In practice, however, Kelemen (2012) finds that chamber variation (using other measures) may be held in check.

The system of chambers at the Court of Justice has evolved over time from an innovation in the Rules of Procedure and some codification in the Treaties back to greater latitude for the Court to self-regulate. Although the membership was ostensibly fixed for two to three years at a time, enlargements, retirements and replacements create more variation even among older cases than the two-year duration would suggest. The features of reorganization and overlap of chambers provides an opportunity to indirectly observe the effects of individual judges' presence on some cases and not others.

By the mid-1980s the Court was deciding many more cases in chambers than in full plenary. The Court had also developed a more complicated system of chambers. In 1986, the Court, preparing for enlargement to 13 members, created six chambers: the first, second, third and fourth chambers consisting of three judges; the first and third combining to create the fifth chamber; and the second and fourth chambers combining to create the sixth chamber.[4] And, in 1986, the Court began to sit in a 'Small Plenum' of seven judges, which was the quorum for decisions by the full Court. This allowed the Court to assign cases to a subset of judges without formally assigning the cases to chambers. As a result, the actual use of the full Court, including all 15 then judges, became rare. By the mid-1990s, less than 20 per cent of ECJ decisions were made by the full Court.

When cases are assigned to different subsets of judges, there is the opportunity for this assignment to affect the outcome of the case. Indeed, Advocate General Francis Jacobs has expressed concern about the very possibility. According to Andenas (1994: fn 54), Jacobs stated that the three-judge chamber 'does not always lead to a consistent practice', and predicted that the five-judge chamber will likely become standard practice, with the more important cases being heard by the full Court. 'Few of our cases are really so trivial,' Jacobs has remarked, 'that they can really ... be entrusted to a three-judge chamber.'

From the late 1970s on, the Court has decided the bulk of cases in chambers. By the early 1990s the Court had the prerogative of assigning any case to chambers, absent a request from a member state or Community institution to have the case heard in plenary. Thus, the internal organization of the Court into chambers certainly allows for a large number of ECJ cases brought under a variety of legal bases to be decided by only subsets of judges sitting in chambers.

A reconstruction of the announced history of judges' assignments to chambers from publication in *Official Journal* from the Preliminary Reference data here (see below) should have between 60 and 80 unique combinations of judges.[5] Instead, the judge-case analysis here 'works' because instead of 80 stable combinations, the decisions studied were made by no fewer than 296 unique combinations of individuals through absences, substitutions and sometimes seemingly *ad hoc* groupings.

STATISTICAL MODEL

The statistical model here connects observed outcomes with latent person and item dimensions, showing variations that I argue arise from judges having heterogeneous preferences. The main claim of this contribution is about the distribution of judge preferences.

The item response model is a standard tool for analysing legislative voting histories and estimating legislators' preferences (Clinton *et al.* 2004; Jackman 2001). Packages such as Jackman's 'pscl' and Martin, Quinn, and Park's 'MCMCpack' (Martin *et al.* 2003) have made item-response models readily usable, and political scientists have brought such methods to bear on a variety of data. Applications in political science have often focused on the ready availability of standard errors for ideal points (Han 2007) and the strength of Bayesian methods with small datasets (Hagemann 2007). Modelled item and subject parameters have been suggested as a way to identify the model, but not generally as parameters of interest themselves (Bafumi *et al.* 2005). A 'hierarchical' model such as the one used here allows us to encode information about units (cases, judges) that distinguish them and therefore distinguish outcomes.

The standard identification strategy for item-response models (e.g., Clinton *et al.* 2004; Høyland 2010; Martin and Quinn 2002) incorporates a small amount of prior knowledge, but not enough in the case of grouped data. I choose to identify the model by case-level predictors. There is intuition about the extremes of cases (such as many member states 'ganging up' against the Commission); the judges have been considered uniform in preference, so there is no ready intuition about the distribution of their preferences. I specify a predictor g of case position that relates to the outcome scale: the number of government observations for and against the Commission.[6]

In a sense, the estimation algorithm turns the model in reverse as it steps through the data to sample the posterior distribution. As we built the model, the result was the outcome Y; as we sample the parameters, we start with Y expanded with participation matrix W, and step through each observation's contribution first to item parameters a and then to judge parameters θ. With the data-level model sampling thus complete, it then proceeds up to the next level of inference, about the distribution of model-level parameters conditional on other prior predictors. Again, at every step the order of sampling (learning from the likelihood contributions of the data) proceeds 'backwards' to greater levels of abstraction or distance from the data.

The details of the model likelihood, prior distributions and convergence are contained in the technical Annex.[7]

DATA AND RESULTS

Data

The data observed comprise a single outcome, attributed to a chamber of judges, per case or legal issue. The dataset was originally coded by Carrubba *et al.* (2008) and separated into legal issues. A complete 'case' before the Court may encompass several legal issues, with a ruling on each of them. Furthermore, observations tendered by the Commission or member states may pertain to one or several legal issues. Legal issues were merged back into complete cases as often as possible, while discarding legal issues lacking Commission participation. In addition, I have parsed the entire electronic record of judgments, and when necessary the printed text, to establish judges' participation on every case since it has been recorded.

The result is a dataset of $N = 1549$ Article 267[8] cases or legal issues – preliminary references – from 1970 to 1997, in which the Commission announced a position via a written observation and argued its position at the hearing. The preliminary reference system provides more than just a steady stream of cases, though. The nature of the cases themselves is more likely, given the confrontational nature of legal proceedings, to lie at the boundary of EU law, and thus presenting the ECJ greater opportunity to expand that boundary. Litigants have incentives to raise points of EU law and creatively interpret it to their advantage. In turn they prompt national court judges to refer questions to the ECJ. This contrasts sharply with direct actions, both by the member states, which engage primarily in actions for annulment, and the Commission, which may under many circumstances hesitate to bring infringement actions targeting member states. The preliminary reference system produces a variety of opportunities to define the boundary of EU law.

These cases were heard by 296 unique combinations of judges; the median number of cases per unique composition of chamber is 2 and the mean 5; the maximum is 95 for the chamber of Judges Zuleeg, Montinho de Almeida and Grévisse.[9]

Overall, the Court sides with the Commission in preliminary references about 75 per cent of the time in the dataset. The model depends on the composition of the chambers deciding against the Commission. Accounting for the participation matrix, judges side with the Commission in these cases from 72 per cent to 85 per cent of the time. Thus, by extension, judges are relatively pro-integration when using the Commission as a proxy of integrationist tendency.

The Commission makes and supports more observations than any other party, but it is frequently joined or opposed by national governments. The position of other member state governments is used to predict the location of the case-specific parameter of the model. If the Court and Commission together are motivated by greater supranational authority, more regulation at the supranational level, and less regulation at the national level – all of these are the components of both positive and negative integration – such a preference will be manifest in case outcomes in which the Court sides with the Commission.

In the data here, about a third have zero net observations; slightly more than half (816) have one and 156 have three.

The observations are revealed to all judges, and are expected to affect all the judges on the chamber uniformly. The net number of observations with respect to the Commission (opposing minus supporting) is used to predict the location of the case parameter in the latent space. *Negative* values of γ would be consistent with the findings in Carrubba *et al.* (2008). It is used to resolve the *reflection invariance* of the model, which means *only* to fix its direction with respect to the outcome (Bafumi *et al.* 2005).

Next, what specific attributes of governing parties are most likely to influence the choice of ECJ judges? Some scholars find that parties take meaningful positions on European integration, in other words that it is a strong 'second dimension' of political competition (Marks and Steenbergen 2004). One of the disadvantages of using manifesto (Budge *et al.* 2001) data is that it offers little in the way of policy domains that amount to 'integration'. It does contain a pair of items for manifesto statements that are positive or negative about the EU; I supplement this with manifesto items about liberalization of trade versus protectionism. Although other problems of comparability or salience of certain issues may arise by using party manifestos, they at least have the property of attaching at the same relative time to the same relative parties that make up governments (Budge 2000; Budge *et al.* 2001; Kim and Fording 2002), as may be the case with surveys.

Although extreme parties of both the Left and the Right often strongly oppose integration, within the mainstream Left parties are consistently more supportive of supranational governance than Right parties (Hix 1999; Hix and Lord 1997). Aspinwall (2002: 82) writes, 'the location of parties and governments in Left–Right space serves as a good independent explanation of preferences on integration'. McElroy and Benoit (2007) find from their own survey of party experts that Left parties tend to favour integration more than Right parties.

I expect that this relationship holds in the judges they would appoint to the ECJ. As a measure of the Left–Right orientation of the government at the time of first appointment, I use cabinet-share weighted manifesto scores from Kim and Fording (2002).

Hypothesis: Judges

If judges share a common uniform preference, resulting estimates will be undifferentiated, or highly dependent on the model prior distribution. For interpretation, the model is specified such that an increase in the value of θ judge position is associated with a greater propensity to decide cases *against* the Commission.

Hypothesis: Judge Predictors

Judges appointed by Right or anti-EU governments will be more likely to decide cases against the Commission. Two separate predictors are used, as discussed above, both derived from cabinet-weighted party positions on both the Left–Right ideological space, and a measure of pro-EU and free trade versus anti-EU and protectionism. In both cases, *positive* values of the parameter β attached to the judge predictor should increase the 'distance' in the latent utility space, resulting in a lower propensity to vote in favour of the Commission.

OTHER EVIDENCE OF JUDGES' HETEROGENEITY

Figure 1 plots the two other measures of judge positions (percentage of cases siding with the Commission and appointing government R–L score from Kim and Fording [2002]). At the left of the figure is the proportion of cases on which each judge participated where the outcome was in favour of the Commission. Even using this aggregate measure, one might conclude that judges' dispositions were not homogeneous. Of course, lacking a model of individual judge and chamber decision-making, one still could not attribute these outcomes to variation in judge preferences.

Results

The chief research question of this contribution is whether the aggregate output of the Court, through chambers composed of individual judges, reveals systematic differences among the member judges. To test this, I model those cases – 1,549 preliminary references – that provide leverage on a few judges at a time. Figures 2 and 3 show the judges' estimated preferences, showing that judges in fact have divergent preferences, and that their imputed policy preferences vary in systematic ways. This result is robust to the precision of the prior and alternative starting values.[10]

Even when we begin with relatively strong or weak beliefs about judge parameters, the data imply a posterior distribution like the one in Figure 2.

The joint distribution of judge preferences in Figure 2 shows evidence that *judges' divergent preferences are evident in the output of the ECJ.* Two types of null result were possible: the distributions could exhibit greater, or even total, overlap; or they could be overly sensitive to the prior information. Figure 3 shows overlap among those judges who most frequently decided together and thus more rarely with other combinations. Overall, most pairwise comparisons show considerable separation. Because we do not observe every possible combination of judges, we learn more about some judges than others. (As noted earlier, the chamber of Zuleeg–Almeida–Grévisse heard more cases together than any other grouping and is thus poorly separated.) The prior expectation would have any pair separable with $p = 0.5$. The data reveal separation in the probability that judges will decide in favour of the Commission, which

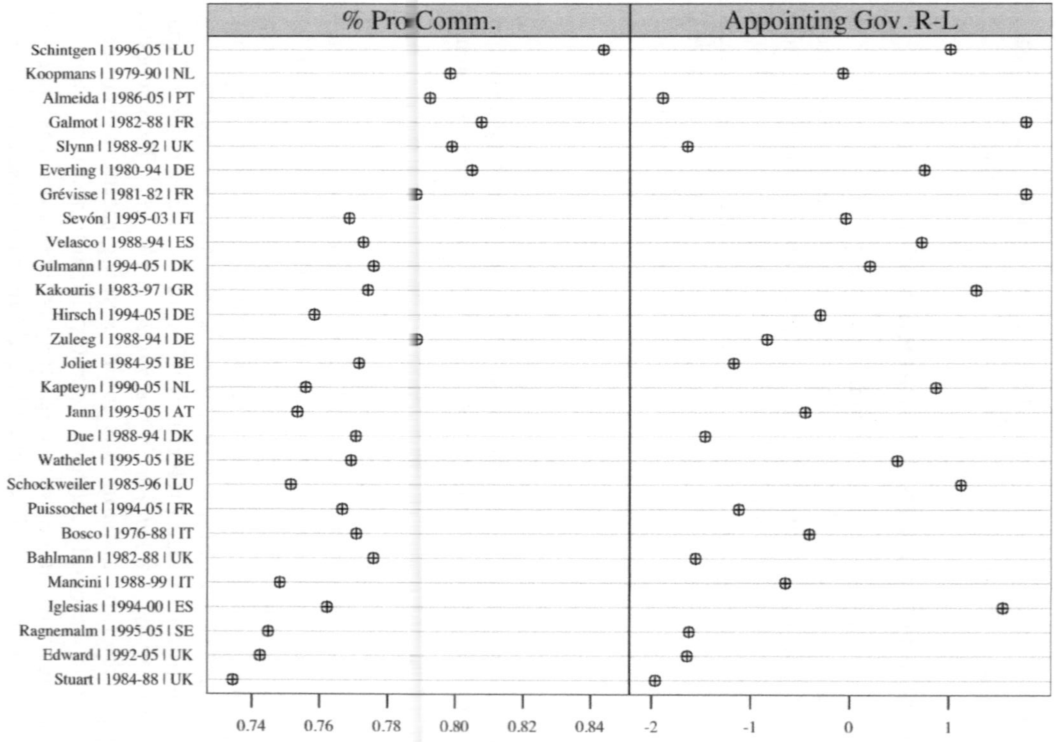

Figure 1 Evidence from judges' aggregate behaviour, and a possible source of heterogeneous motivations on the bench: the percentage of cases each judge heard in any chamber in which the outcome favoured the Commission; and the Right–Left ideology of their national government at the time of their appointment. The latter is used as a predictor in the hierarchical model.

Notes: The scale is reversed so that right or conservative governments are associated with Eurosceptical judges. The ordering is the same as in Figure 2.

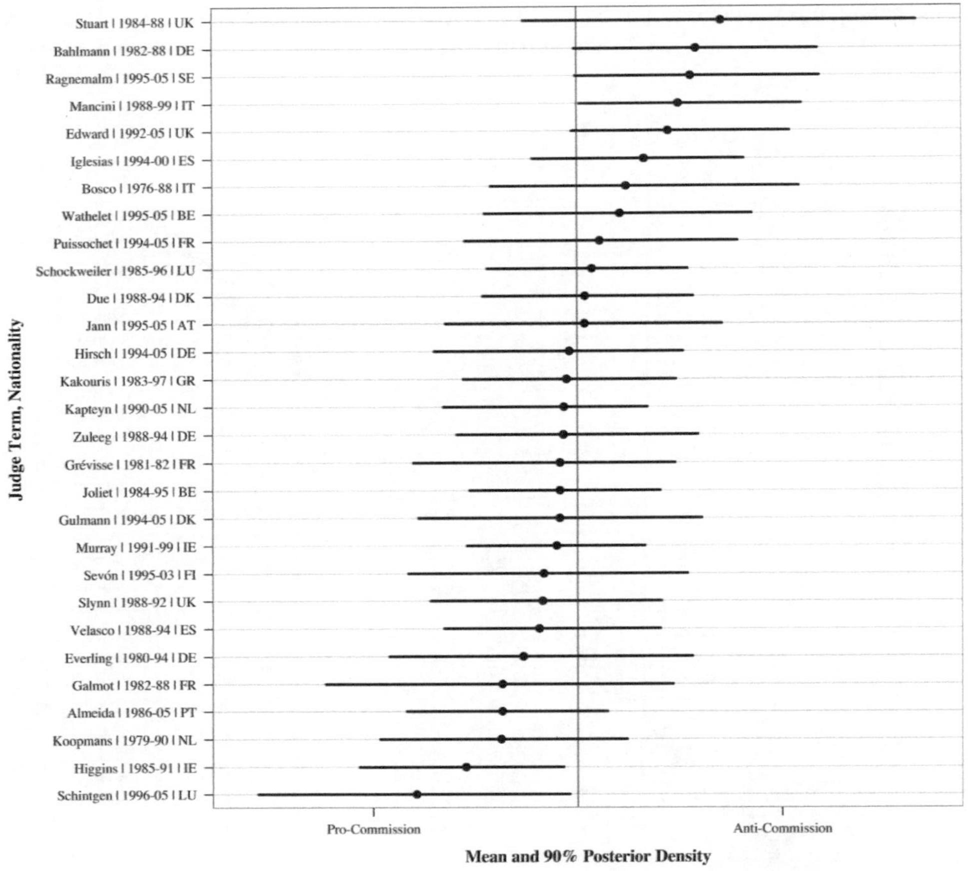

Figure 2 Estimated ECJ judge positions (θ) from ecological item response (eco-irt) model.

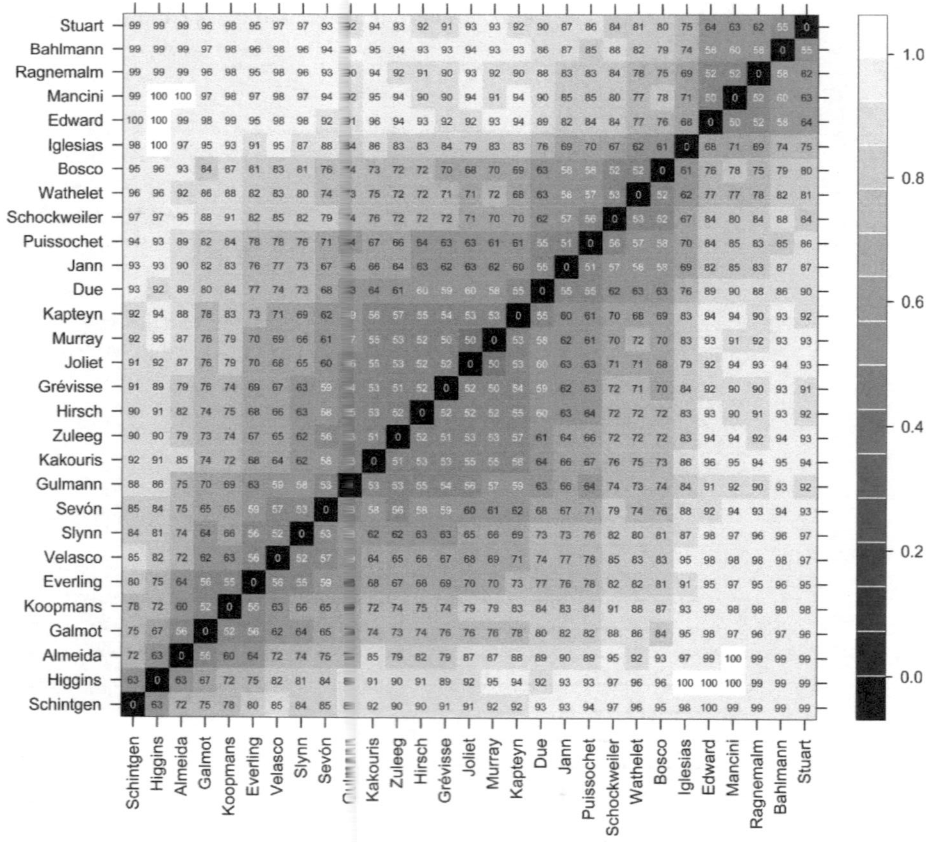

Figure 3 The matrix of pairwise comparisons of judges' preference estimates.
Note: Numbers indicate the degree of certainty of the ranking of the row relative to the column. Even though both ends of the joint distributions in Figure 2 – Judges Schintgen and Mackenzie Stuart – overlap each other, this figure shows 99 per cent certainty that they diverge.

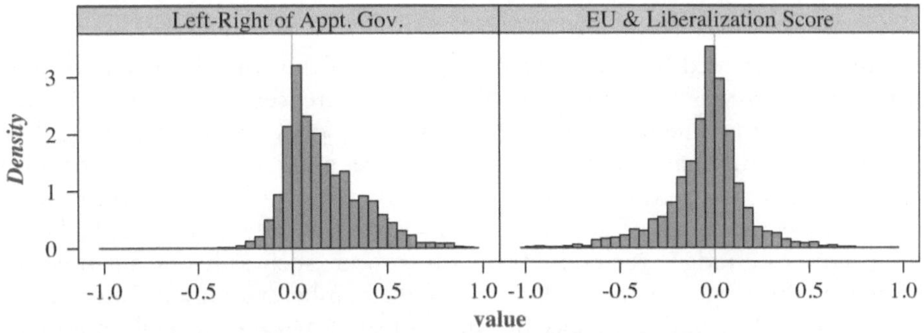

Figure 4 Posterior density plots of two prior predictors of judges' preferences.

supports the claim that their underlying preferences on this dimension *are not uniform.*

As predicted, the ECJ's insulation has provided equal cover to relative Eurosceptics and Europhiles alike.

The wide, overlapping bands in Figure 2 understate just how much information the model has actually recovered from the permutations of chambers. Figure 3 shows that although joint distributions may overlap considerably, the ordering is, with some exceptions, reasonably well defined.

Figure 4 shows two covariates to predict judge behaviour: the Left–Right cabinet median discussed earlier, and a similar cabinet median of a similar normalized index of two other items coded in the Comparative Manifesto Project dataset: position (positive or negative) on the European Communities/European Union, and position on liberalization versus protectionism.[11]

Because of its institutional insulation from the member states and the other supranational institutions, the ECJ can affect policy with few constraints. The claim has two parts: first, judges' motivations are homogeneous (they all prefer integration to roughly the same degree); and second, they develop this preference endogenously on the court.

In response to the first question – do judges reveal observable patterns of heterogeneous preferences? – yes, though, as in most item-response models, the positions of adjacent judges are sometimes ambivalent.

The second part of the claim that judges have a common preference for integration is more subtle. It suggests that their behaviour would reveal such motives regardless of the preferences of the member states. If this were true, there would be no systematic relationship between judges' behaviour and the preferences of member state governments that appoint them. Instead, they are weakly correlated with the Left–Right composition of government at the time of initial appointment, and they show no relation to the manifesto-based government integration measure.

CONCLUSION

The model presented here uses the organization of the court into chambers of various compositions to infer individual judges' preferences. In particular it is presently difficult to evaluate the effects of individual judges on particular cases. For any case, we would have to specify a new chamber and compute the probability that the outcome would differ; this raises the question of how to constitute a new chamber in terms of size and membership. An alternative would be to bring more case-judge-specific information to bear, such as his or her time on the bench at hearing, and the presence of his own member state among interveners, and perhaps other judge-case-specific effects of the Advocate General's opinion.

To date, little research has conceptualized the court as a collection of individuals each with interests and preferences. The complex interactions of national politics, integration and enlargement offer a rich vein for future research.

Biographical note: Michael Malecki is Postdoctoral Research Scholar in the Applied Statistics Center and Department of Political Science at Columbia University.

NOTES

1 Directive 95/46/EC, OJ L 281, 23/11/1995, pp. 31–50.
2 European Commission, 'The Commission's Agent in Court' available at http://ec.europa.eu/dgs/legal_service/agent_en.htm (accessed 15 May 2010).
3 Even then, only on cases relating to intellectual property as determined by the Treasury Solicitor of the UK. See 'Handling of cases before the Court of Justice of the European Union', available at http://www.ipo.gov.uk/pro-policy/policy-information/ecj/ecj-refs.htm, Intellectual Property Office, United Kingdom (accessed 16 April 2010).
4 Because the EEC Treaty permitted only chambers of three or five judges, the fifth and sixth chambers sat with only five of the six members of their constituent lower chambers.
5 Some uncertainty arises when judges left the ECJ before to the end of their term. Sometimes seats on the chamber were left empty and decisions taken in their absence. Sometimes one or more members of the Court heard one or more cases in their place.
6 Bafumi *et al.* (2005) recommend this method of identification and it is discussed, but not implemented, in Martin and Quinn (2002). Gabel *et al.* (2007) use it for both identification and inference.
7 The technical annex can be found at http://sites.google.com/site/malecki/jepp-ecj-appendix (last accessed 27 September 2011).
8 Ex Article 234; ex Article 177.
9 Larger configurations of 7, 9, 11 or 13 judges (the *petit plenum, grand plenum*, and quorum of the full court) have also existed but were used far less frequently and not at all after the 2005 reform of the Rules of Procedure. The model, of course, is agnostic of formal membership in chambers or the order of rotation; for all (and

only) the judges hearing a given case, a case makes a contribution to judges' estimate if they are coded as 1 in the participation matrix.

10 Hyperprior parameters are given weakly informative *t* distributions with low degrees of freedom, and the variance is set at 10 and 100 producing 'weakly informative priors' (Gelman 2006; Gelman and Hill 2006; Gelman *et al.* 2004, 2008).

11 This alternative 'integration index' is available at the same level of precision (all countries in all years) as the Manifesto-based Left–Right index. It correlates weakly with the L–R measure and identifies the same countries as being 'anti-integration' as expert surveys that only classify parties/governments into three categories.

REFERENCES

Alter, K.J. (2001) *Establishing the Supremacy of European Law: The Making of an International Rule of Law in Europe*, New York: Oxford University Press.

Andenas, M. (ed.) (1994) *Article 177 References to the European Court: Policy and Practice*, London: Butterworths.

Aspinwall, M. (2002) 'Preferring Europe: ideology and national preferences on European integration', *European Union Politics* 3(1): 81–111.

Bafumi, J., Gelman, A., Park, D.K. and Kaplan, N. (2005) 'Practical issues in implementing and understanding Bayesian ideal point estimation', *Political Analysis* 13(2): 171–87.

Bobek, M. (2008) 'Learning to talk: preliminary rulings, the courts of the new member states and the court of justice', *Common Market Law Review* 45(6): 1611–43.

Börzel, T.A. (2003) 'Guarding the treaty: the compliance strategies of the European Commission', in T.A. Börzel and R.A. Cichowski (eds), *The State of the European Union, Volume 6; Law, Politics and Society*, Oxford: Oxford University Press, pp. 197–220.

Börzel, T.A., Hofmann, T. and Panke, D. (2009) *Opinions, Referrals, and Judgements: Analyzing Longitudinal Patterns of Non-compliance*, Berlin: Freie Universität Berlin.

Budge, I. (2000) 'Expert judgements of party policy positions: uses and limitations in political research', *European Journal of Political Research* 37(1): 103–13.

Budge, I., Klingemann, H.-D., Volkens, A., Bara, J. and Tanenbaum, E. (2001) *Mapping Policy Preferences: Estimates for Parties, Electors, and Governments, 1945–1998*, Oxford: Oxford University Press.

Carrubba, C.J., Gabel, M. and Hankla, C. (2008) 'Judicial behavior under political constraints: evidence from the European Court of Justice', *American Political Science Review* 102(4): 435–52.

Cichowski, R.A. (1998) 'Integrating the environment: the European court and the construction of supranational policy', *Journal of European Public Policy* 5(3): 387–405.

Cichowski, R.A. (2001) 'Judicial rulemaking and the institutionalization of European Union sex equality policy', in A. Stone Sweet, W. Sandholtz and N. Fligstein (eds), *The Institutionalization of Europe*, Oxford: Oxford University Press, pp. 113–36.

Cichowski, R.A. (2004) 'Women's rights, the European Court, and supranational constitutionalism', *Law & Society Review* 38(3): 489–512.

Cichowski, R.A. (2007) *The European Court and Civil Society: Litigation, Mobilization and Governance*, Cambridge: Cambridge University Press.

Clinton, J., Jackman, S. and Rivers, D. (2004) 'The statistical analysis of roll call data', *American Political Science Review* 98(2): 355–70.

Gabel, M.J., Hix, S. and Malecki, M. (2007). 'From preferences to behavior: modeling MEPs' roll-call voting behavior', Paper presented at *Midwest Political Science Association Annual Meeting*, Chicago, 4–7 April.

Garrett, G. (1995) 'The politics of legal integration in the European Union', *International Organization* 49(1): 171–81.
Gelman, A. (2006) 'Prior distributions for variance parameters in hierarchical models', *Bayesian Analysis* 1(3): 515–33.
Gelman, A., Carlin, J., Stern, H. and Rubin, D. (2004) *Bayesian Data Analysis*, 2nd edn, Boca Raton, FL, London and New York: Chapman & Hall/CRC.
Gelman, A. and Hill, J. (2006) *Data Analysis Using Regression and Multilevel/Hierarchical Models*, Cambridge: Cambridge University Press.
Gelman, A., Jakulin, A. and Grazia, M. (2008) 'A weakly informative default prior distribution for logistic and other regression models', *The Annals of Applied Statistics* 2(4): 1360–83.
Granger, M.-P. (2006) 'States as successful litigants before the European Court of Justice', *Croatian Yearbook of European Law and Policy* 2(2): 27–48.
Hagemann, S. (2007) 'Applying ideal point estimation methods to the council of ministers', *European Union Politics* 8(2): 279–96.
Han, J.-H. (2007) 'Analysing roll calls of the European Parliament: a Bayesian application', *European Union Politics* 8(4): 479–507.
Hartley, T. (2007) *The Foundations of European Community Law: An Introduction to the Constitutional and Administrative Law of the European Community*, 6th edn, New York: Oxford University Press.
Héritier, A. (2001) 'Overt and covert institutionalization in Europe', in A. Stone Sweet, W. Sandholtz and N. Fligstein (eds), *The Institutionalization of Europe*, Oxford and New York: Oxford University Press, pp. 56–70.
Hix, S. (1999) 'Dimensions and alignments in European Union politics: cognitive constraints and partisan responses', *European Journal of Political Research* 35(1): 69–106.
Hix, S. and Lord, C. (1997) *Political Parties in the European Union*, Basingstoke: Palgrave Macmillan.
Høyland, B. (2010) 'Procedural and party effects in European Parliament roll-call votes', *European Union Politics* 11(4): 597–613.
Jackman, S. (2001) 'Multidimensional analysis of roll call data via Bayesian simulation: identification, estimation, inference, and model checking', *Political Analysis* 9(3): 227–41.
Kelemen, R.D. (2012) 'The political foundations of judicial independence in the European Union', *Journal of European Public Policy* 19(1): 43–58.
Kim, H. and Fording, R.C. (2002) 'Government partisanship in Western democracies, 1945–1998', *European Journal of Political Research* 41(2): 187–206.
Marks, G. and Steenbergen, M.R. (eds) (2004) *European Integration and Political Conflict*, Cambridge: Cambridge University Press.
Martin, A.D. and Quinn, K.M. (2002) 'Dynamic ideal point estimation via Markov Chain Monte Carlo for the US Supreme Court, 1953–1999', *Political Analysis* 10(2): 134–53.
Martin, A.D., Quinn, K.M. and Park, J.H. (2003) MCMCpack: Markov Chain Monte Carlo (MCMC) package. R package version 0.9-5, available at http://mcmcpack.wustl.edu (accessed 7 September 2011).
Mattli, W. and Slaughter, A.-M. (1995) 'Law and politics in the European Union: a reply to Garrett', *International Organization* 49(1): 183–90.
Mattli, W. and Slaughter, A.-M. (1998) 'The role of national courts in the process of European integration: accounting for judicial preferences and constraints', in A.-M. Slaughter, A. Stone-Sweet and J.H.H. Weiler (eds), *The European Court and National Courts – Doctrine and Jurisprudence*, Oxford: Hart, pp. 253–76.
McElroy, G. and Benoit, K. (2007) 'Party groups and policy positions in the European Parliament', *Party Politics* 13(1): 5–28.

Rasmussen, H. (1986) *On Law and Policy in the European Court of Justice: A Comparative Study in Judicial Policymaking*, Dordrecht: Martinus Nijhoff.
Rasmussen, H. (1998) *The European Court of Justice*, Copenhagen: GadJura.
Slaughter, A.-M., Stone Sweet, A. and Weiler, J. (eds) (1998) *The European Court and National Courts – Doctrine and Jurisprudence: Legal Change in its Social Context*, Oxford: Hart.
Stein, E. (1981) 'Lawyers, judges, and the making of a transnational constitution', *American Journal of International Law* 75(1): 1–27.
Stone Sweet, A. and Brunell, T.L. (1998) 'Constructing a supranational constitution: dispute resolution and governance in the European Community', *American Political Science Review* 92(1): 63–81.
Weiler, J. (1994) 'A quiet revolution: the European Court of Justice and its interlocutors', *Comparative Political Studies* 26(4): 510–34.
Wiklund, O. (ed.) (2003) *Judicial Discretion in European Perspective*, Stockholm: Norstedts Juridik/Kluwer Law International.

Activism relocated. The self-restraint of the European Court of Justice in its national context

Gareth Davies

ABSTRACT Most cases involving EU law are decided in national courtrooms without a preliminary reference. The influence of the Court on these cases is often overstated by focusing on headline principles, such as mutual recognition and state liability. However, application of these principles in specific cases is often mediated by open norms such as proportionality, which allow much national court discretion. Whether national judges apply these open norms in a pro-integration way determines how far the broader principles directly impact on the national legal system, and on national regulators: these latter will condition their behaviour according to their expectations of the national judiciary, since these are the judges to which they are directly subject. The Court's role here is important, but limited. It enables and encourages pro-integration national judicial choices, but its case law does not compel them. Claims of activism need to be partly relocated from Luxembourg to national courts.

INTRODUCTION

The two central elements of the role of the Court of Justice in European integration are the interplay between its judgments and the European Union (EU) political process, and the impact of those judgments on national law, legal systems and regulators. Within scholarship about the latter the degree to which the Court imposes integration in a way that could be described as 'activist' has been a recurring question (Arnull 1996; Craig 2011; Hartley 1996; Rasmussen 1986). In answering this, as in more general analysis of the character and influence of the Court, the primary evidence examined has tended to be the substantive principles expressed in its judgments and the consequences that the particular judgments have for the parties and states involved. However, most EU law is applied by national courts, and most cases in which EU law is relevant will never be heard or ruled upon by the Court (Conant 2003). The direct influence of the Court within national legal systems largely depends on the extent to which it influences these national judgments. Even the Court's influence on the national legislator will be partly mediated by how its judgments are understood and applied by national courts (Alter and Meunier-Aitsahalia 1994; Wasserfallen 2010: 1133).

This contribution aims to complement studies of other aspects of the Court's role and influence by offering a theoretical exploration of the relationship between Court of Justice judgments and national judgments applying EU law in national courts. It does not ask how the Court answers substantive questions, about which much has been written, but to what extent those answers influence or determine the outcome of cases where no question is asked. It does not make empirical arguments about any such influence, but draws on law and theory to construct an argument about what kind of influence is to be expected.

The suggestion made is that it is too simple to assume that because the Court has answered questions on, for example, healthcare or citizenship in far-reaching and pro-integration ways that national courts must do the same. On the contrary, two aspects of EU law give national courts considerable freedom to pursue their own path and express their own values and opinions. The first of these is proportionality, and other similarly open norms which are central to many areas of EU law. The ambiguity of these norms has the consequence that they leave a significant discretionary space for the court applying them (Kumm 2010; Stone Sweet and Mathews 2008). It has been noted that the Court itself, when referred a question, often uses this space to intervene disruptively and controversially in national legal orders (Martinsen 2011). In its hands, the malleability of proportionality allows it to be moulded into a tool for integration. However, this very same malleability, and the resulting discretionary space, makes it possible for a national court of different views to take a restrictive approach, to find national measures justified, necessary and proportionate, and to read EU law in a weaker way.

The second relevant aspect of EU law is the preliminary reference procedure, and the procedural rules which the Court has developed concerning it. These influence the degree to which the Court is able, in practice and in principle, to over-rule or pre-empt national court judgments on proportionality, and therefore the extent to which national court discretion is constrained. In practice, it will be suggested below, the chances of a reference in a given case are relatively small, and it is moreover possible for a national court to structure their judgment in a way which makes it hard for the Court to disagree with them – by using the national court monopoly over findings of fact to define the context in a certain way. In principle, the Court itself repeatedly emphasizes that findings of proportionality are context- and fact-specific and ultimately for the national judge alone.[1] While this principle sits somewhat uncomfortably with the actual practice of the Court in its judgments – it does delve remarkably into the facts at times – the existence and repeated confirmation of the principle provide a doctrinal excuse for national judges, particularly final judges, to avoid references and safeguard decisions from Court of Justice interference.

The picture of the Court which emerges is nuanced. It has certainly formulated principles of law which require a fundamental rethink of many aspects of national legal orders. However, it has also formulated substantive conditions and procedural rules which together pass the primary responsibility for that rethinking to national courts, with only limited Court-imposed constraints on how the resulting discretion is used.

This perspective has been under-emphasized in scholarship on the relationship between the Court and national courts, perhaps because that scholarship has been dominated by the early Court doctrines of supremacy and direct effect. The challenge for the Court was to insert these doctrines into national legal orders. Hence, the emphasis in the scholarship on the *acceptance* of EU law, particularly by national supreme courts, but also by the national judiciary in general (Alter 2001; Stone Sweet 2004; Weiler 1991).

By contrast, there is relatively little attention in the legal or political science literature for exactly what that acceptance might entail. That does not matter too much where supremacy and direct effect are concerned, since these are quite simple and absolute rules. However, in substantive and administrative EU law more nuanced rules of law are found, in which open norms are central, and here the question *how* the law is used becomes at least as important as *whether* it is used, and a focus on acceptance can mislead. These areas of law involve balancing between competing interests and policies, and factual specificity is often crucial to decisions. The dynamic of the relationship between the Court and national judges is here less to do with acceptance of doctrine and more to do with how they share an ill-defined discretionary interpretative space.

This contribution begins its argument with an outline of the distinct functions allocated to national courts and the Court of Justice within the preliminary reference procedure. It then examines how the open norms which are widely prevalent in EU law may blur the lines between these functions. The next part shows how practical and legal factors make it possible for national judges to exploit this ambiguity to entrench their views and preferences, and resist control by the Court. The final parts consider how EU law may achieve pro-integration effects within national legal systems, and reassess the degree to which causality should be attributed to the Court or to the substantive preferences of national judges.

THE DIVISION OF FUNCTIONS IN THE PRELIMINARY REFERENCE PROCEDURE

The preliminary reference procedure envisages a division of functions and powers between the national court and the Court of Justice. The national court may ask the Court to interpret and explain EU law, but only the national court may apply that interpretation to the facts or national law in issue (Article 267 TFEU). The Court of Justice has no competence to rule on the conformity of national measures with EU law, nor on any other aspect of the facts or context of the case.

This distinction has been repeatedly reiterated by the Court of Justice over the years, and is uncontroversial as a question of principle.[2] Nevertheless, it does not prevent the Court from commonly providing very concrete answers to questions. It will often take an explicit view on whether a measure is in fact justified, or whether a state has shown that a measure is necessary, so that the 'application' of this answer by the national court is merely a formality (Cohen 1996; Davies 2006). Insofar as the Court is indicating what types of arguments, interests and values may be considered, and how they are to be weighed and balanced, even such a concrete answer can be seen as a legitimate part of its interpretative function (Bengoetxea *et al.* 2001). However, the danger is that it makes assertions of fact or national law – that a given measure will not harm consumers, or the finances of the welfare state, or the interests of workers, or the environment, or that a given national rule has a certain effect, for example – which are outside its jurisdiction and competence, and where the national court, upon hearing evidence, might legitimately come to a different conclusion. In that case, its trespass upon the national applicatory monopoly becomes a potential source of conflict (Arnull 2003; Davies 2003).

A widespread view of the Court's concrete approach to answering references is that it is helpful to the national judge, since it provides clearer and more certain guidance as to how they should decide the case than would mere abstract propositions. Moreover, insofar as the Court comments on fact and national law it must rely on the dossier sent to it by the national court, so its views will often be aligned with those of the referring judge. Nevertheless, the situation can arise where a national judge finds that the Court's view of some evidential matter is incorrect, and then, as the English Court of Appeal in *Arsenal v Reed* found, it is open to the national court to ignore that part of its answer.[3] The Court's view on the meaning of the Treaty and other EU law is binding, but its comments on how these apply to a particular case, while often helpful, are not.

In general, national courts have discretion whether to refer a question or whether to interpret and apply EU law without one (Article 267 TFEU). However, final courts, beyond which no appeal is possible, are obliged to refer all questions of EU law which it is necessary to decide in any case before them (*ibid.*). In principle, this ensures that any party may gain access to the Court of Justice, and to an authoritative determination of EU law, by continually appealing within the national system. However, the scope of this obligation depends on the degree to which a question is seen as one of interpretation of EU law, or of its application. As will be discussed below, this distinction is sufficiently ambiguous to effectively allow national supreme courts discretion in many cases: they could certainly refer if they wanted to, but they could also legitimately argue that, for example, the proportionality of a given measure is purely a question of application.

OPEN NORMS AND NATIONAL COURT DISCRETION

The prevalance of open norms

Four areas of EU law which are of great social and legal importance, and where the Court has been accused of activism, are free movement, non-discrimination law, the rules pertaining to the interpretation of directives and the law on damages for breach of EU law (Betlem 2002; Cichowski 2004; Granger 2007; Scharpf 2002; Slepcevic 2009). In all of these areas, the central legal concepts are imprecise ones, which are open to varying interpretations. In free movement and discrimination law it is proportionality which is central. Measures tending to disadvantage the foreign economic actor, the foreign citizen or the under-represented sex, race or religion will be prohibited unless they serve a justified goal and are proportionate.[4] What is proportionate in each case is of course a highly contested question (Kumm 2010). In the law pertaining to directives, the law is that national law must be interpreted 'so far as possible' in conformity with a directive, without going so far that the clear meaning of the law is contradicted (*Marleasing*: C-106/89). Clearly, both the notions of the clear meaning and of a possible interpretation are also highly open (Betlem 2002). Finally, the law on damages requires that these be paid for 'sufficiently serious' breaches of EU law (*Brasserie du Pecheur*: C-46/93 and 48/93). Both the concepts of 'so far as possible' and of 'sufficiently serious' involve an inherent balancing between the systemic requirements of legal certainty and practical operation, and on the other hand, the imperative to enforce EU law. The outcomes of cases turn, as with proportionality, upon decisions about the weight to be given to various interests, yet the principles themselves do not determine that relative weight. It is possible, in good faith, to come to different conclusions on the application of these norms to specific cases, with the result that they leave individual judges the room to incorporate their personal values or perspectives in their ruling.

The ambiguity in these areas of law is a common feature of EU law, which in part results from the open and incomplete nature of the bargain represented by the Treaty (Stone Sweet 2004). The member states made an imprecise deal, for reasons of political and legal expedience, and are faced with imprecise legal consequences. However, the openness of the norms also has to do with the context in which EU law is applied. When national measures are assessed for legality under national law there is invariably a conflict between an individual, pleading his rights and interests, and the policy-maker, pleading broader considerations. Since the nature of majoritarian democracy is such that individual rights serve only as an outer constraint on the legislator, national judicial review tends to be procedural, formal and not particularly intrusive. By contrast, when national measures are assessed for legality under EU law, the conflict is at least in part between two legitimate legislators – the national and the European – and their policy priorities. This is, to a far greater degree, a policy-balancing process, with all the fact-specific ambiguity which this entails (Kumm 2010; Stone Sweet and Mathews 2008; van Gerven 1999).

This is not to say that the open norms in EU law are entirely unstructured or bounded. The Court has provided guidelines which determine the outcome of some classes of case. It has provided a number of conditions concerning state liability, such as the ruling that failure to implement a directive is always sufficiently serious (*Dillenkofer*: C-178/94). In some areas, notably free movement and discrimination law, it regularly finds not just that a given measure is disproportionate but that measures of a certain type cannot be proportionate, essentially structuring and filling-in proportionality (*Laval*: C-341/05). Nevertheless, much space remains, and in many situations the conclusion on proportionality, seriousness or the possibility of a conforming interpretation is not pre-determined either by previous cases or by general principles, but is a case-specific finding.

In recent years it has been commented that the Court has shown some inclination to proceduralize proportionality, as is common in national legal traditions of judicial review (Prechal 2008; Semmelman 2010). Rather than itself second-guessing the balance of interests which the national legislator or judge has made, the Court has displayed a tendency to consider whether the national body has followed the right steps: has it considered the relevant interests, has it paid them thorough attention, and has it provided reasoning for its conclusions? This structuring is helpful to both national regulators and judges, since it provides them with a – fairly rough – 'compliance guide'. However, it may be noted that proceduralization entrenches, more than it diminishes, substantive discretion, since following the correct procedure rarely dictates any particular outcome. Insofar as a procedural approach to proportionality takes root at the Court, national authorities and judges will be essentially granted a process whereby they can legitimate – in the eyes of EU law – their own preferences.

Mixing fact and law

The open norms mentioned above share the characteristic that any application of them is not just the application of a rule of law but also a finding of fact (Davies 2006; Kumm 2010). Whether a measure is proportionate depends upon the meaning of proportionality, and on the specific facts surrounding that measure. They are therefore highly context-specific norms. A national judge may accept the principle of mutual recognition as derived from *Cassis de Dijon (*120/78), but nevertheless come to the conclusion that the particular national measure she is faced with is in fact necessary, and is in fact proportionate, and therefore not in conflict with the Treaty. These norms leave room for particularism, and are only weakly constraining (Stone Sweet and Mathews 2008). Reinterpreting *Cassis de Dijon* in this light one could say that it does not create a rule of mutual recognition, but the opportunity for such a rule. It does not require national judges to disapply national product standards, but *enables* them to. Ultimately, whether they do or not depends upon their particular view of whether the particular rule in question is sufficiently justified by some important reason of public policy. In fact, it has been noted that national judges have been rather good at finding reasons to justify national measures, so that the enforceability of mutual recognition in national courts is more limited than the confident and abstract phrasing of the *Cassis* judgment might suggest (Jarvis 1998; Pelkmans 2003).

The extent to which Court judgments explicitly delegate the last word to national judges varies, for reasons which remain under-explored in the literature (Davies 2006; De Burca 1993). In some cases the Court states quite explicitly that only the national judge is competent to assess the proportionality of the measure in question. *Viking Line* (C-438/05), *Bressol* (C-73/08) and *Rottmann* (C-135/08) are recent examples which have attracted attention. In the first of these the Court ruled that union action against posted workers could violate free movement law, creating some concern about EU law threatening the right to strike. In the second the Court had to consider whether Belgium could restrict the inflow of foreign medical students in response to fears that they would all return home upon graduation and leave the country with a shortage of doctors. The issue was of great importance to Belgium, whose higher education system faces quite some pressure from migrating Dutch and French students. In *Rottmann* the Court found that withdrawal of national citizenship could, under some circumstances, be contrary to the Treaty since it could lead to loss of EU citizenship. The case is regarded as of principled importance as an intervention in national citizenship law, and the decision could be of practical impact if it is used to prevent states adopting laws stripping immigrants who commit crimes of their new nationality. Yet, in each of these cases, the Court explicitly found that the legality of the measures depended upon whether they were justified by legitimate aims and proportionate, which was a factual question to be decided by the national judge alone. That is, of course, equally true of similar disputes which may arise in the future. Application of the doctrines is explicitly decentralized and left indeterminate.

In other cases the discretionary role of the national judge is more implicit. *Ruiz Zambrano* (C-34/09) is a recent citizenship case in which the Court found that Belgium was obliged to grant the Colombian Mr Ruiz Zambrano a work and residence permit, simply because his child was Belgian. The Court found that a failure to grant the permits would force him, and therefore his child, to leave the EU, depriving the child of the most basic EU citizenship right – the right to live in the EU. If the case means that the third-country parents of EU citizen children automatically have a right of residence and work in the EU, then it has potentially dramatic consequences for national immigration law, not least because it is unclear whether the ruling applies to the situation where one parent is European and the other is not, which is relatively common. However, a central plank of the judgment is the Court's view that the Belgian denial of rights to Mr Ruiz Zambrano would effectively force him and his child to leave the EU. Whether or not correct in the particular case, it may not be in others. Each family drama has its own nuances, and national judges may be reluctant to conclude that the departure from Europe of EU-citizen children is a necessary corollary of measures taken against their parents. This could depend not only on the parent–child relationship but also on alternative carers and the national attitude towards, and possibilities for, alternative forms of care. How sacred is the family? Legal systems vary in the degree to which they regard separating parent and child as acceptable, and under which circumstances. The activist national judge has been given sufficient tools by the Court of Justice to justify rewriting national immigration law but has sufficient leeway to avoid this if they wish.

In many other cases the Court makes it apparently harder for the national judge to follow their own path. In *Laval* (C-341/05), a case similar to *Viking* which was decided just a week later, or in the string of important cases on patient mobility (*Geraerts-Smits*: C-157/99, *Müller-Fauré*: C-385/99), the most prominent example perhaps being *Watts* (C-372/04), the Court worded its decisions in a way which appears to leave little or no discretion to the national judge, simply stating that measures of the type in question were contrary to the Treaty. This would seem to tie the hands of judges in similar cases, as well as the referring judges.

However, while these cases provide clear prohibitions, they do so only for certain specific kinds of measure. The reality is that the measure addressed by *Laval*, or the healthcare cases, are but a small selection of the ways in which unions, posted workers and the labour market, or patient mobility and healthcare systems, may interact. The complexity of the policy fields involved, and the inevitable legal and systemic peculiarities attaching to any particular case or national system, may well mean that these case are distinguished more often than they are followed. That is not to say that national judges may not overrule aspects of national labour law or healthcare regulation, but that in most cases they will be applying their own findings on proportionality rather than merely being bound by the findings of the Court.

The cases show the structural limitations of the Court's power over national courts. On a reference it can provide an answer which essentially decides on justification and proportionality, and so determines the outcome of the case, but to do this inevitably entails engagement with the specificities of the case, making that answer easier for other judges to distinguish, and less generally applicable. Alternatively, it can answer in abstractions and general principles, providing rules of wide application, but in doing so it must accept that its answers merely guide the national judge, but do not control outcomes. If it tries to finesse this choice, by providing general rules which are also determinative, for example by ruling that broad classes of measures simply cannot be justified, then it risk accusations that it has pre-empted inherently factual and contextual questions, and thereby not just interpreted but applied the law and exceeded its jurisdiction. By allocating judicial functions using the somewhat artificial and unclear distinction between fact and law, interpretation and application, the reference procedure creates a balance of power which it is hard for the Court to escape.

SYSTEMIC CONSTRAINTS ON NATIONAL COURT DISCRETION

The threat of appeal to the Court

A factor constraining national judicial discretion may be the possibility that parties will appeal and ultimately force a reference to the Court. In principle it is open to any party to force a reference in any case involving EU law simply by appealing within the national system to the final court, which is then obliged by Article 267 TFEU to refer. A Eurosceptic judge might be deterred from applying open norms in a way deferential to national measures by the fear that he will in effect be reversed by a later reference. In practice, however, this is unlikely, and so not much of a constraint.

Firstly, there is unlikely to be such a reference. The costs involved are significant, and many litigants will also be deterred by the two or three years that a reference may take. References occur in a minority of cases (Conant 2003). Even if the case is appealed to the final court a reference may well not occur. Although the general rule is that such a court must refer any non-trivial question concerning the interpretation of EU law which comes before it and is relevant to the case outcome, it is not unusual for a final national court to avoid this by taking the view that the correct interpretation of the law is not in doubt (the Court of Justice has exempted such obvious cases from the obligation to refer; *CILFIT*: 283/81) (Arnull 2002: 187). The only thing required, it is sometimes claimed, is to apply that law to the facts of the case – for example, to decide on the proportionality of a measure – which is a national court matter and not suitable for a reference.

One might have expected the Court of Justice to close this 'loophole', which anecdotal evidence among lawyers suggests is very widely used. It has had opportunities both in the past and recently, notably in *Köbler* (C-224/01), to address the issue of precisely when a final court must refer, and it might have ruled, for example, that the proportionality of a measure is, as a question of mixed law and fact, something that must be referred. It is notable that it has chosen not to do this – workload may be a factor here – and not to clarify the issue in any way at all (Davies 2006), preserving the ambiguity and, hence, the discretionary space which final courts enjoy. This reduced chance of a final court reference should be expected to have a trickle-down effect on lower courts, increasing their 'protection' from a subsequent reference, and thus emboldening them to apply EU law narrowly, should they be so inclined.

The national judicial monopoly on fact-finding also provides an opportunity for a national judge to tie the hands of the Court in the event that a later reference does in fact occur. If the national court has already made certain findings of fact, for example that a certain measure is necessary to achieve a given policy goal, or is practically impossible, or would have certain consequences, then these constrain the Court significantly in its decision on proportionality. There is evidence that courts formulate their questions strategically for this kind of reason, and have some success in extracting the answers that they want from the Court (Nyikos 2006). That is unsurprising: it is hard for the Court to contradict the national court on such factual matters. To do so creates the risk that the national court will 'evade' application of the Court's answer by reinterpreting the facts (Nyikos 2003), or, worse, that the national court will claim that the ECJ has exceeded its jurisdiction (Arnull 2003). This famously happened in *Arsenal v Reed*, where an English judge refused to follow part of an answer from the Court, because it concerned the facts and was, in his view, outside the Court's jurisdiction (Arnull 2003; Davies 2003). While the Court of Appeal found the lower judge had misunderstood the Court of Justice, and over-ruled his judgment, it did also confirm the principle that national courts could reject answers from the Court insofar as these trespassed on the domain of fact.[5] This example serves as a reminder that the Court is dependent upon national judges and has good reasons to be sensitive to the division of functions between them. Indeed, where the Court does answer questions concretely, and take a view on the facts, it is more plausible to explain this in terms of assistance to and co-operation with the national court – as a response to their request for concrete help – than as an attempt to dominate or control them. The next section expands on this.

Finally, both national courts and regulators may be constrained by the possibility of an enforcement action by the Commission. Such an action would bring the state of EU law application in the member state directly before the Court of Justice, giving it the opportunity to decide whether it accepts the approach to application which national courts have been following. This is certainly a factor relevant to decision-making at the national level, but it is also relevant to note that such actions tend to occur only when breaches of EU law are significant, the actions are relatively slow, and states are given a warning period first, during which they may avoid the action by changing their behaviour (Kapteyn *et al.* 2008: 441-446). Most importantly, the precedents for enforcement actions based on misapplication of the law by judges are very few, and are not based on misjudgment of proportionality or open norms (*Köbler*: C-224/01, *Traghetti del Mediterraneo*: C-173/03, *Commission v Italy*: C-129/00). Such an action would be a contentious and path-breaking stretching of the line between the competences of the Court and national courts.

Contextual differences between national cases and those before the Court of Justice

For the reasons discussed above, compulsory references from final courts do not comprise the majority of references. Most references come from lower courts, who refer as a matter of discretion (Arnull 2002). They are free to take their own view on a claimed conflict between national law and EU law, or to ask the Court.

A number of cultural and institutional factors have been proposed which may make reference more or less likely (Alter and Vargas 2000; Conant 2001; Martinsen and Wind 2010). However, the nature of the case and the preferences of the individual judge may also be expected to play a role. A judge has more motivation to refer if they take the view that a national measure is contrary to the Treaty than if they take the view that it is not. EU law contains a more substantive standard of review than most national legal traditions, and national judges, particularly lower national judges, may often feel nervous about taking their view to its conclusion and over-ruling national law and policy (Alter 2001). Apart from going against the spirit of their judicial training and tradition, the chances of appeal within the domestic system are high, so they risk being called to order by a higher court, bad both for their self-respect and career (Lasser 2003). They may understandably seek the support and protection of a reference.

This explains the concrete nature of many of the Court's answers. For a national judge faced with a specific national measure, it is more supportive if the Court provides an indication of the legality of that measure than if it tenders an abstract framework of principle. Judges, it is often said, want answers to their questions, and they usually frame their questions concretely; is measure X contrary to the Treaty? The Court, anxious to help and not to alienate national judges, gives them what they want, even though this may stretch the Treaty-imposed division of powers (Arnull 2002; Nyikos 2006). By contrast, a national court which does not want to set aside a national rule has more reason to decide the case themselves, without a reference (Cohen 1996: 427; Golub 1996). Since the Court is known to take a relatively pro-integration view of matters, a reference is likely to deny the national judge their preference instead of supporting it.

Finally, because references are such a slow and costly exercise, it is unlikely that a litigant will wish to push for a reference unless they believe that they have a good chance of winning. Cases where the reasons to maintain the national measure are strong are therefore less likely to be referred, and so are likely to be represented in national courts to a greater extent than a simple survey of Court of Justice decisions might first suggest.

RELOCATING ACTIVISM

The Court of Justice as an activist court

Claims that the Court of Justice directly imposes its view of the law on member states become much weaker when one looks at how EU law works in national courts. There is so much discretion remaining that the imposition is more formal than real. National courts are required to take EU law into account, and to acknowledge certain principles, but their ultimate findings in many areas of this law will continue to depend on the approach to balancing and the preferences of the national judge in question, or the national legal system constraining that judge (Wasserfallen 2010: 1142f.).

Looking at EU law in national courts also requires us to rethink views on the character of the Court. That its doctrines are partly smothered by national discretion is not unavoidable. It could have done a lot more to push national judges into applying proportionality and the other open norms in pro-integration ways (Davies 2006). It has not done so, repeatedly confirming the factual autonomy of the national judge, and failing to intervene where national final courts have taken a limited stance on the obligation to refer. The only evidence that it has any 'activist' agenda – any desire to impose its own agenda on EU law – is in its own tendency to take pro-integration positions when it is asked by a national court to judge a particular case. But the fact that these are but a small percentage of EU law cases, and of limited precedential value, limits the impact of this, while any light that it casts on the Court must be filtered through the fact that it is only doing what national judges ask it to: they refer concrete questions, in situations where it is overwhelmingly likely that they want answers facilitating the over-ruling of a member state measure. The Court does promote integration when it answers these questions, but its behaviour is that of an agent at least as much as it is that of a principal.

National activism and risk-aversion

Yet EU law does sometimes have a surprising impact. If it is true that many important cases have not been effectively translated into general doctrines, it is also true that in some member states there have been fundamental reorganizations of aspects of the market, the state and the legal system in response to EU law (Scharpf 2002; Stone Sweet 2010). If the responsibility of the Court for this process is often over-stated (Wasserfallen 2010), then it may be worthwhile to ask where else that responsibility could be placed.

The analysis of EU law offered in this contribution suggests two mechanisms whereby EU law could still have dramatic effects within member state legal systems, beyond what is textually inevitable. The first is via the national judiciary, who may choose, as a matter of discretion, to use the tools which EU law offers them in a particular way and to rule against restrictive national measures in favour of EU policies. It has been suggested that one reason why they might do this is because EU law offers lower judges the chance to assert themselves against higher ones (Alter 2001; Golub 1996). However, other factors may be important, too. Most obviously, the judiciary may authentically perceive that national measures are unduly or unnecessarily restrictive and serve no particular goal. Alternatively, they may place a higher value on European integration than the average citizen, or be more inclined towards the preferences that EU law embodies (regulatory liberalism, control of the state, non-discrimination) than the average citizen is and so be inclined to reach results which are controversial among the general population. Or, there may be more complex aspects of professional identity at work: judges may have a strong preference to integrate legal systems and avoid conflicts or tensions between them in the striving for a coherent whole. Pro-integration judgments may be motivated by the lawyer's preference for systemic coherence more than substantive policy ideas.

The second mechanism which may lead to integrationist results is via national regulatory authorities. Once again, they may be voluntarily using EU law in a pro-integration way because it coincides with their own strategic agendas – for deregulation, or re-regulation, or autonomy from the central government, for example. However, an equally important, but conceptually quite different, factor behind pro-integration choices by national regulatory authorities is likely to be risk-aversion (Greer and Rauscher 2011; Sabel and Simon 2004). Regulators like certainty, and will try to create systems which are safe from legal challenge. This is not merely a question of the mentality of the civil servant, but of efficiency and good sense; successful legal challenges cause chaos and are expensive and disruptive. Where norms are uncertain and the law is unclear, there may therefore be a tendency among regulators to act defensively and take pre-emptive 'restabilizing' measures to avoid legal challenge. However, it should be noted that since such legal challenge primarily takes place in national courts, the foundation for such defensive behaviour is a perception that national judges are in sympathy with the Court of Justice and are unlikely to find justifications to save national measures where these impede EU goals (Nyikos 2003). If regulators are confident that the national judiciary will take a limited view of EU law, then they will be emboldened to do so themselves.

In either case, therefore, it is the fact or appearance of national judicial alignment with EU policy which serves to generate national alignment with that policy. If judges are protective of national measures and quick to find them justified, and are perceived to be protective, such national adjustments will take place to a lesser extent. National judicial discretion is central to the reach of EU law within the member states.

CONCLUSION

The image of the Court presented here is as relatively restrained. It offers powerful substantive principles to national judges, but continues to respect and accept considerable national court discretion in how these are applied. Why does the Court take this approach? Why does it not push national courts to resolve national–EU legal conflicts in an integrationist way?

One reason may simply be the preferences of judges in Luxembourg. As nationally schooled lawyers, national citizens, Europeans and, in most cases, temperamental conservatives they are unlikely to want an over-centralized EU or the crushing of national autonomy, institutions and concerns. The qualification of EU law's consequences by reference to the national legal and factual circumstances will in many cases reflect their view of a just interpretation of the law.

In some cases it may also reflect a strategic agenda. The Court may be aware that the ultimate success of EU law depends on national judicial support, and that excessive bossiness and doctrinal overreach could be counterproductive (Rasmussen 1986; Weatherill 2003). Classic texts on European integration repeatedly emphasize the non-hierarchical nature of the preliminary reference procedure, and the view when it was created was always that hierarchy must be avoided at all costs (Kapteyn *et al.* 2008: 479). The Court needed the sympathy and co-operation of national judges if EU law was to be effective, and this would be undermined if it seemed to be dominating them, rather than supporting them. Hence it would answer questions to help them decide cases themselves, but it would not tell them what to do. The Court has maintained that spirit to a remarkable extent.

Looked at in this way, the most apparently far-reaching and controversial judgments may not always be the most effectively integrationist. They may pronounce much, but achieve little. The internal market is an example. The widespread consensus that legal and bureaucratic obstacles to movement continue to be significant (Alter and Meunier-Aitsahalia 1994; Majone 1995; Pelkmans 2003) gives the lie to any suggestion that the principles of *Cassis*, *van Binsbergen* (33/74), *Corsten* (C-58/98), *Gebhard* (C-55/94) and other cases have fully been realized in the member states. The breadth and depth of their principles may have been too much for national courts to digest.

One consequence of the Court's tolerance of national discretion is that it is a less effective partner-in-integration for the Commission. This body often uses the concepts expressed in the Court's case law in its proposals for secondary legislation, and to some – disputed (Nowak 2010) – extent therefore the Court may guide the shape of legislation. Yet, if those concepts only give a partial and over-rosy picture of what EU law means in the national legal systems, then building them into legislation is likely to result in ineffective law. This is, in a nutshell, the criticism often made of the new approach to harmonization. The Commission believed that mutual recognition as created in *Cassis* would render much harmonization unnecessary and devised plans for an efficient and minimalist legislative program. That this did not result in open markets is largely because mutual recognition did not in fact work as a simple reading of *Cassis* might suggest that it would. The doctrinal basis for this failure is in the legal points discussed above.

Biographical note: Gareth Davies is Professor of European Law (Department of Transnational Legal Studies) at the VU University of Amsterdam.

NOTES

1 *Costa v ENEL*: 6/64, *Shipping and Forwarding*: C-320/88, *Fratelli Graffioni*: C-313/94, *Gourmet International*: C-405/98, *Torfaen*: C-145/88, *Mickelsson and Roos*: C-142/05, *Viking*: C-438/05, *Carmen Media*: C-46/08.
2 See note 1 above.
3 *Arsenal Football Club v Matthew Reed* [2003] 2 CMLR 25; [2003] EWCA Civ 96, Aldous LJ at 25-26.
4 *O'Flynn*: C-237/94, Directive 2000/43 Article 2, Directive 2000/78 Article 2, Directive 2006/54 Article 2.
5 See note 3 above.

REFERENCES

Alter, K.J. (2001) *Establishing the Supremacy of European Law: The Making of an International Rule of Law in Europe*, Oxford: Oxford University Press.

Alter, K.J. and Meunier-Aitsahalia, S. (1994) 'Judicial politics in the European Community: European integration and the pathbreaking "Cassis de Dijon" decision', *Comparative Political Studies* 26(4): 535–61.
Alter, K.J. and Vargas, J. (2000) 'Explaining variation in the use of European litigation strategies', *Comparative Political Studies* 33(4): 452–82.
Arnull, A. (1996) 'The European Court and judicial objectivity: a reply to Professor Hartley', *Law Quarterly Review* 112: 411–23.
Arnull, A. (2002) 'The past and future of the preliminary rulings procedure', *European Business Law Review* 13(3): 183–91.
Arnull, A. (2003) 'Annotation of *Arsenal v Reed*', *Common Market Law Review* 40(3): 753–69.
Bengoetxea, J., MacCormick, N. and Soriano, L.M. (2001) 'Integration and integrity in the legal reasoning of the European Court of Justice', in G. De Burca and J.H.H. Weiler (eds), *The European Court of Justice*, Oxford: Oxford University Press, pp. 43–86.
Betlem, G. (2002) 'The doctrine of consistent interpretation: managing legal uncertainty', *Oxford Journal of Legal Studies* 22(3): 397–418.
Cichowski, R. (2004) 'Women's rights, the European Court, and supranational constitutionalism', *Law and Society Review* 38(3): 489–512.
Cohen, J.C. (1996) 'The European preliminary reference and US Supreme Court review of state court judgments: a study in comparative judicial federalism', *American Journal of Comparative Law* 44(3): 421–61.
Conant, L. (2001) 'Europeanization and the courts: variable patterns of adaption among national judiciaries', in M.G. Cowles, J.A. Caporaso and T. Risse (eds), *Transforming Europe – Europeanization and Domestic Change*, Ithaca, NY: Cornell University Press, pp. 97–115.
Conant, L. (2003) *Justice Contained: Law and Politics in the European Union*, Ithaca, NY: Cornell University Press.
Craig, P. (2011) 'The ECJ and Ultra Vires action: a conceptual analysis', *Common Market Law Review* 48(2): 395–437.
Davies, G. (2003) 'Of rules and referees: Arsenal v Reed', *European Law Review* 28(3): 408–17.
Davies, G. (2006) 'Abstractness and concreteness in the preliminary reference procedure', in N.N. Shuibhne (ed.), *Regulating the Internal Market*, Cheltenham: Edward Elgar, pp. 210–44.
De Burca, G. (1993) 'The principle of proportionality and its application in EC law', *Yearbook of European Law* 13: 105–50.
Golub, J. (1996) 'The politics of judicial discretion', *West European Politics* 19(2): 360–85.
Granger, M.-P. (2007) 'National applications of Francovich and the construction of a European administrative IUS commune', *European Law Review* 32(2): 157–92.
Greer, S.L. and Rauscher, S. (2011) 'Destabilization rights and restabilization politics: policy and political reactions to European Union healthcare services law', *Journal of European Public Policy* 18(2): 220–40.
Hartley, T.C. (1996) 'The European Court: judicial objectivity and the Constitution of the European Union', *Law Quarterly Review* 112: 95–109.
Jarvis, M. (1998) *The Application of EC Law by National Courts: The Free Movement of Goods*, Oxford: Oxford University Press.
Kapteyn, P., McDonnell, A.M., Mortelmans, K. and Timmermans, C.W.A. (eds) (2008) *Kapteyn and Verloren van Themaat: The Law of the European Union and the European Communities*, 4th edn, The Hague: Kluwer.
Kumm, M. (2010) 'The idea of Socratic contestation and the right to justification: the point of rights-based proportionality review', *Law and Ethics of Human Rights* 4(2): 141–75.

Lasser, M. (2003) 'Anticipating three models of judicial control, debate and legitimacy: the European Court of Justice, the Cour de Cassation, and the United States Supreme Court', *Jean Monnet Working Paper 1/03.*

Majone, G. (1995) 'Mutual trust, credible commitment and the evolution of the rules of the single market', *EUI RSC Working Paper 95/01.*

Martinsen, D.S. (2011) 'Judicial policy-making and Europeanization: the proportionality of national control and administrative discretion', *Journal of European Public Policy* 18(7): 944–61.

Martinsen, D.S. and Wind, M. (2010) 'When national courts go to Europe: reluctant or active players in the integration process?' in H. Koch, K. Hogel-Sorensen, U. Haltern and J.H.H. Weiler (eds), *Europe. The New Legal Realism*, Copenhagen: DJØF Publishing, pp. 479–500.

Nowak, T. (2010) 'Of garbage cans and rulings: judgments of the European Court of Justice in the EU legislative process', *West European Politics* 33(4): 753–69.

Nyikos, S.A. (2003) 'The Preliminary Reference Process', *European Union Politics* 4(4): 397–419.

Nyikos, S.A. (2006) 'Strategic interaction among Courts within the Preliminary Reference Process – Stage 1: National court pre-emptive opinions', *European Journal of Political Research* 45(4): 527–50.

Pelkmans, J. (2003) 'Mutual recognition in goods and services: an economic perspective', *ENEPRI Working Paper 16/March 2003* (Brussels: European Network of Economic Policy Research Institutes), available at www.ceps.eu/ceps/download/867

Prechal, S. (2008) 'Free movement and procedural requirements: proportionality reconsidered', *Legal Issues of Economic Integration* 35(3): 201–16.

Rasmussen, H. (1986) *On Law and Policy in the European Court of Justice. A Comparative Study in Judicial Policymaking*, Dordrecht: Martinus Nijhoff.

Sabel, C.F. and Simon, W.H. (2004) 'Destabilization rights: how public law litigation succeeds', *Harvard Law Review* 117(4): 1015–101.

Scharpf, F.W. (2002) 'The European social model: coping with the challenges of diversity', *Journal of Common Market Studies* 40(4): 645–70.

Semmelman, C. (2010) 'The European Union's economic constitution under the Lisbon Treaty: soul searching among lawyers shifts the emphasis to procedure', *European Law Review* 35(4): 516–41.

Slepcevic, R. (2009) 'The judicial enforcement of EU law through national courts: possibilities and limits', *Journal of European Public Policy* 16(3): 378–94.

Stone Sweet, A. (2004) *The Judicial Construction of Europe*, Oxford: Oxford University Press.

Stone Sweet, A. (2010) 'The European Court of Justice and the judicialization of EU governance', *Faculty Scholarship Series, Paper 70*, available at http://digitalcommons.law.yale.edu/fss_papers/70 (accessed 7 September 2011).

Stone Sweet, A. and Mathews, J. (2008) 'Proportionality balancing and global constitutionalism', *Columbia Journal of Transnational Law* 47(1): 73–165.

Van Gerven, W. (1999) 'The effect of proportionality on the actions of member states of the European Community: national viewpoints from continental Europe', in E. Ellis (ed.), *The Principle of Proportionality*, Oxford: Hart, pp. 37–63.

Wasserfallen, F. (2010) 'The judiciary as legislator? How the European Court of Justice shapes policy-making in the European Union', *Journal of European Public Policy* 17(8): 1128–46.

Weatherill, S. (2003) 'Activism and restraint in the European Court of Justice', in P. Capps, M. Evans and S. Konstadinidis (eds), *Asserting Jurisdiction: International and European Legal Perspectives*, Oxford: Hart, pp. 255–81.

Weiler, J. (1991) 'The transformation of Europe', *Yale Law Journal* 100(8): 2403–83.

Rights adjudication and constitutional pluralism in Germany and Europe

Alec Stone Sweet and Kathleen Stranz

ABSTRACT The development of a corpus of fundamental rights at the EU level has accentuated the constitutional pluralism that existed within many national legal systems. Illustrating the dynamic, the adjudication of the age discrimination provisions of the 2000 Framework Directive on Employment Equality in Germany produced two major outcomes. First, interactions between the ECJ and the German labour courts served to upgrade rights protections afforded to workers, relative to national constitutional standards. Second, the structural position of the German Federal Constitutional Court, as a privileged locus of rights protection, was weakened, while the authority of the labour courts was enhanced. Looking ahead, we are entering a new era of rights-based legal integration that will further serve to Europeanize national law, while undermining the (supposed) unity and coherence of national legal orders.

INTRODUCTION

This article builds on two strains of research on the European Court of Justice (ECJ) and legal integration.[1] The first tracks and evaluates the impact of the ECJ's case law on market and political integration. The scholarship has conclusively shown that the legal system of the European Union (EU) has pushed integration further than member states were prepared to go on their own, under extant decision-rules, provoking a process of adaptation on the part of EU legislators and national officials (Cichowski 2007; Mattli and Slaughter 1998; Stone Sweet 2004). A second strain has documented the interactions of the ECJ and the national courts (Alter 2001; Nyikos 2003; Panke 2007), processes resulting in the gradual 'Europeanization' of national legal orders. Our focus here is on the judicial politics of rights protection, specifically on how German courts and the ECJ have interacted to create and enforce a right to be free from discrimination in the workplace.

The case study is important in its own right. Adjudicating the 2000 Framework EU Directive on Employment Equality produced two linked outcomes. First, it consolidated the rights-based, 'constitutional pluralism' that characterizes the German legal system. By 'constitutional pluralism', we refer to a situation, within the domestic legal system, in which two or more sources of judicially enforceable rights, occupying a rank above statute, co-exist.[2] Second, private litigants, German labour judges, and the ECJ leveraged EU fundamental rights to upgrade German standards of rights protection to a higher, European level, marginalizing the German Federal Constitutional Court (GFCC) in the process.

The wider significance of the case also deserves emphasis. Kelemen (2011) has demonstrated that the importance of the ECJ and the national courts broadly expanded as the EU's legislative bodies (post-Single European Act) embraced a rights-based, court-centric system for monitoring and enforcing member state compliance with EU secondary law. This contribution provides further empirical support for Kelemen's arguments. With respect to the themes developed by the editors of this collection (Kelemen and Schmidt 2012), we do not see the importance of the ECJ and the national courts declining in the near future. On the contrary, the expansion of broad judicial review powers in the service of rights protection will reinforce the legal system's capacity to control outcomes.

The case study we present is embedded in crucial legal developments that have taken place over the past four decades (Bell 2011). In the 1970s and 1980s, the ECJ developed a general principle of equality – in the guise of a fundamental right to be free of discrimination – through its rulings on equal pay and equal treatment of the sexes. By the end of the 1990s, the Court's jurisprudence on non-discrimination had thoroughly 'judicialized' EU law-making in the area, all but requiring the EU's legislative organs to codify the Court's major rulings as entrenched secondary law (Cichowski 2001). These rulings also opened up new domains of national policy to the reach of EU law through national judges. Most important, they obliged national courts to supervise workplace rules and practices, that is, private contractual relations. A new wave of activity began in 2000, when the EU legislator initiated a series of rights-based secondary legislation that, in effect, codified the (in part, unwritten) general principle of equality that the Court had elaborated. The most important of these statutes is Directive 2000/78 – 'establishing a general framework for equal treatment in employment and occupation'. In *Mangold* (C-144/04), a momentous 2005 ruling, the ECJ 'constitutionalized' the provisions of the Directive related to age discrimination, by holding that the Directive's main features expressed norms that already existed as (unwritten) EU fundamental rights. The *Mangold* saga heralds a new generation of inter-court, judicial politics that will heavily condition how the European system of rights protection will evolve.

The contribution is organized as follows. Section 2 provides an overview of how EU equality law had developed prior to the *Mangold* ruling. We then (3) discuss long-standing tensions within German law, as embodied in the differing approaches of the German Federal Labour Court (GFLC) and the GFCC to the application of rights in disputes between private parties. Section 4 focuses on the *Mangold* litigation and its consequences. As Sections 2–4 show, the development of EU equality law undermined the autonomy of the national legal order, while enhancing constitutional pluralism within Germany. In the conclusion (5), we argue that the distinctive architecture of rights-based constitutionalism in Europe, coupled with the EU's turn toward combating discrimination will further undermine the (supposed) unity and coherence of national legal orders, while bolstering the importance of the relationship between the ECJ and the national courts.

THE ECJ AND THE CONSTITUTIONALIZATION OF NON-DISCRIMINATION

Beginning in the late 1970s, the ECJ began to 'constitutionalize' the notion of sex equality. In *Defrenne II* (43/75), the Court recognized the direct effect of ex-Art. 119 EC (now Art. 157 TFEU), which obliges the member states to ensure that men and women receive 'equal pay for equal work', thus converting that provision into a right that individuals could ask national courts to enforce. Over two decades, the scope of this right steadily expanded to include much more than salary and wages. During this same period, the Court also developed the 'general principle of equality' from two sources: ex-Art. 119 EC and the 1976 Equal Treatment Directive. Gradually, a justification for this jurisprudence emerged. The EU, the Court stressed, was not just an economic association to be legitimated through efficiency-based rationales. It was also a social community, whose duty it was to mitigate at least some of the injustices generated in market and workplace relations.

As scholars have extensively documented (Bell 2011; Ellis 1998, 2005; Stone Sweet 2004: ch. 4), the constitutionalization of sex equality made the courts the site of normative innovation, largely eclipsing legislative authority at both the EU and national levels. The Commission leveraged the ECJ's rulings, using them as templates for new EU statutes, including directives on indirect discrimination (1997), occupational social security (1986) and pregnancy and maternity (1996). The general outcome – recurrent codification of the Court's progressive case law – flows in part from the fact that the ECJ treated the norm of non-discrimination as a fundamental right, conferring upon it a higher-law position within the structure of EU law.

For present purposes, the '*constitutionalization* of the principle of non-discrimination' refers to several overlapping features of equality law.[3] A first concerns legal sources. In 1980, it could be assumed that a discrete piece of secondary legislation, the 1978 Equal Treatment Directive, comprised the source of the principle of equal treatment of the sexes, and that ex-Art. 119 EC originated the rule that men and women must receive equal pay for equal work. By the end of the 1990s, the Court had made it clear that these texts expressed norms of equality and non-discrimination which could also be found in the (judge-made) general principles of EU law. A second feature relates to the procedure through which the member states, or governments, may override the Court's jurisprudence in this area. Normally, an unwanted interpretation of a treaty provision or a statute may be overridden, respectively, through treaty revision (by a unanimous vote of the member states) or statutory amendment (in this domain, the override rule would be a unanimous vote on the part of governments acting in the Council of Ministers). It is not at all clear, however, how the member states could override the Court's case law on fundamental rights (the general principles), even if they could muster consensus. A third characteristic of the principle of equality must also be stressed. As a fundamental right, it is imbued with both vertical and horizontal direct effect, a point that warrants further discussion.

In the 1960s, the Court famously initiated its 'constitutional' jurisprudence of direct effect and supremacy (Mancini 1989) which, as national courts adapted to it, would gradually but inexorably 'transform' the EU (Weiler 1991), federalizing the regime in all but name (Lenaerts 1990). Treaty provisions and directives that meet certain criteria are directly effective; that is, private parties may plead them at national bar. The central purpose of such litigation is to provoke judicial scrutiny of member state compliance with EU law. Individuals, firms and groups generate the case load; the preliminary reference procedure (governed by Art. 267 TFEU) organizes a dialogue between the ECJ and the national courts on issues concerning the conformity of national law to EU Law; and, under the doctrine of supremacy, the national judge must set aside (disapply) any national legal rule or practice that conflicts with EU law. In areas governed by direct effect and supremacy, national judges are expected to act as agents of the EU legal order, not the national order.

The ECJ took an aggressive stance with respect to the *vertical direct effect of EU law*, which refers to the immediate judicial applicability of EU law to disputes between (a) private parties and (b) national organs of government. As the Court has consistently stressed, direct effect constitutes a mechanism for enhancing 'the effectiveness' of EU law within national legal orders. The doctrine has been central to market-building through 'negative integration', the judicially led process through which barriers to intra-EU trade in goods and services, labour flows and investment are removed (see Schmidt 2012). When adjudicating cases involving one of the 'four freedoms', vertical direct effect was enough. The Court's position on the *horizontal direct effect of EU law*, which refers to the applicability of EU law to relations between two private persons or entities, was more nuanced. In *Defrenne II*, the Court opened the door to horizontal direct effect, holding that, under the Treaty, employers could not operate systems of remuneration that discriminated on the basis of sex. By virtue of the direct effect of ex-Art. 119 EC, employees may bring suit against employers before national judges, thereby triggering judicial review of the firm's workplace policies, as well as the national law that would permit such policies. Adjudicating disputes under EU law that is applicable between private parties inevitably implicates judges in 'positive integration', the process through which EU law, designed to replace disparate national regulation, is made and applied. Somewhat controversially (Prechal 1995), the ECJ has balked at conferring horizontal direct effect on directives that member states had either failed to transpose into national law, or had transposed incorrectly.[4]

Here, again, we encounter features of legal doctrine that are crucial to our analysis. Most important, the general principles, including fundamental rights, enjoy at least the rank of Treaty law in the hierarchy of legal norms of the EU. The Court, therefore, can recognize the *horizontal direct effect* of a fundamental right. In the domain of sex equality, the ECJ has on several occasions held that norms found in EU statutes simply reflect a higher-law norm embedded in the general principles. When it does so, statutory law is effectively 'constitutionalized', and *horizontal direct effect* kicks in. Thus, while the ECJ constrained the reach of judicial authority in denying the horizontal direct effect of directives, it may overcome this constraint through determining that a fundamental right is in play. If, from the perspective of the ECJ's 'constitutional' jurisprudence, national courts are agents of the EU legal order every time they adjudicate disputes in domains governed by EU law, then a crucial point follows. Once the Court decides that an EU legal norm is possessed of horizontal direct effect, by virtue of its relationship to a fundamental right, national constitutional rights and the jurisprudence of national constitutional courts are no longer dispositive.

The question of whether national judges actually conform to the role that the ECJ has imagined for them – as faithful 'agents' of EU law – is not merely a doctrinal question but a deeply political one. After all, national judges may consider themselves to be, first and foremost, agents of the national legal order; national rights jurisprudence may dictate outcomes that the ECJ, under the supremacy doctrine, would require them to abandon; and the ECJ has no direct means to compel national courts to comply with its rulings. As an empirical matter, the question will be settled on the basis of choices made by specific national judges in specific cases. The ECJ's equality jurisprudence broke new ground;[5] indeed, it has been transformative. Outside of EU law, for example, the concept of indirect sex discrimination *per se* was unknown in the law of the member states.[6] Some national judges were initially reticent about adjudicating such cases, and some initially rejected the (alien) doctrinal framework that the Court developed to deal with claims of indirect discrimination, a version of an intrusive form of scrutiny called *proportionality analysis.* Gradually, however, judges did adapt to the Court's case law with wide-ranging consequences for national conceptions of equality and discrimination that are still being worked out.

Member states governments too adapted: they ratified the Court's moves, codifying the Court's case law in directives (Stone Sweet 2004: 159–70). The doctrinal framework governing the adjudication of indirect discrimination, for example, is found (copied virtually word-for-word) in a provision of the 1997 directive on the matter, further facilitating its diffusion within national orders. In 1999 (Treaty of Amsterdam), the member states provided legal basis for legislation serving to combat discrimination (now Art. 19.1 TFEU), upon the unanimous vote of the Council with the consent of the Parliament.

In 2000, legislators adopted the Framework Directive on Employment Equality (2000/78/EC), part of a 'suite' of 'secondary rights legislation' that would soon appear (Bell 2011). The Directive prohibits discrimination in employment, benefits and work conditions based on age, disability, religion, belief and sexual orientation. The legislation explicitly references the Court's established case law; it covers both direct and indirect discrimination, as well as harassment; and it is directly applicable, upon transposition, both vertically and horizontally. With the Framework Directive, the EU's legislative branch had harnessed judicial authority to make the principle of non-discrimination effective at the level of the workplace. Indeed, it made obligatory the ECJ's preferred methodology: proportionality analysis of any public interest or economic justification that would infringe upon the principle of non-discrimination. Proportionality analysis involves least-restrictive means testing and balancing (discussed further below); adopting it constitutes, in effect, a rejection of judicial deference to political or economic decision-makers in favour of a strict form of review (Stone Sweet and Mathews 2008).

In sum, the Directive provided the basis for a significant incursion of EU law into national law and workplace practices. Unavoidably, national judges would be faced with deep, structural choices about the nature of and scope of the authority of the EU and of the ECJ. In the next two sections, we focus on how German courts have made these choices, with what systemic consequences.

RIGHTS PLURALISM IN GERMANY

When it comes to rights protection under the Basic Law, the German legal order is characterized by a structural condition: constitutional pluralism (defined above).[7] Perhaps contentiously, we do not view the German legal order as a unified normative system, or German rights doctrine as coherent. In many EU member states (Stone Sweet 2009), rights-based pluralism means that two or more high courts, with respect to the same litigants (or class of litigants), can claim authority to resolve legal disputes about the scope, content and applicability of a right, and no single high court can directly impose its authority on the other(s). In Germany, apart from the GFCC, there are five, autonomous supreme courts; some of these routinely enforce functionally equivalent rights provisions under the jurisprudence of the GFCC, the ECJ, and the European Court of Human Rights; and the mechanism developed to ensure the GFCC's control over how the other domestic supreme courts adjudicate rights claims – the individual constitutional complaint – has proved to be inadequate when it comes to European law. Moreover, some German courts self-consciously use the ECJ to enhance their own authority, and to subvert that of the GFCC (Alter 2001).

In fact, constitutional pluralism emerged in the early years of the Federal Republic, when the GFLC moved to give horizontal direct effect to the rights provisions of the Basic Law. To our knowledge, the GFLC was the first court to do so anywhere in the world. In a series of seminal rulings, the GFLC held that rights, including of speech and conscience, marriage, sex equality, and human dignity and personality, were directly applicable between employees and employers.[8] By 1957, the GFLC could treat the horizontal direct effect of rights as settled case law.[9] The move was controversial. It imported, into the 'private law', norms that were considered to be part of the 'public law', obliterating distinctions many considered to be foundational. In developing this jurisprudence on its own, without a reference to the GFCC, the GFLC also implicitly denied the GFCC's centrality as the fount of rights protection. The outcome, the construction of rights as binding on relations between employers and employees, was unanticipated by the founders of the Federal Republic (Quint 1989: 252–58).

In 1958, the GFCC reacted, in its celebrated *Lüth* ruling.[10] The GFCC held that, since the 'constitutional values' (now usually called 'principles') permeate 'all spheres of law', it was the duty of the entire judiciary to ensure the compatibility of 'every provision of the private law' with rights. The Court rejected two 'extreme' positions: the view that rights are exclusively norms of the public law, and do not touch the private law; and the position taken by the GFLC on the horizontal direct effect of rights in employment law. *Lüth* took a middle road, standing for the proposition that the rights enumerated in the first chapter of the Basic Law (Arts. 1–19) are *indirectly effective* between individuals: in consequence, judges are obliged to interpret the various codes that make up the private law as if these codes had been written in conformity with rights provisions (as interpreted by the GFCC on an ongoing basis). The *Lüth* ruling provoked a long series of battles between the GFCC and the Supreme Civil Court (*Bundesgerichtshof*), as the GFCC worked to 'constitutionalize' the Civil Code, while civil judges sought to defend their autonomy. The GFLC continued down its own path, usually managing to stay one step ahead of the GFCC. To circumvent the GFCC's control, for example, the GFLC strengthened what is now known as the General Clause on Equality, an expansive, unwritten, judge-made right to be free of discrimination in workplace relations, which the GFLC had originated prior to *Lüth*.[11] Thus, significant constitutional pluralism existed in Germany prior to the advent of the ECJ's equality jurisprudence.

Unlike the GFLC, the Constitutional Court had chosen not to give equality a privileged status (Fuchsloch 1995; Kokott 1995). Art. 3.1 of the Basic Law comprises a general equal treatment clause; Art. 3.2 provides equal rights between women and men; and Art. 3.3 prohibits discrimination on the grounds of sex, parentage, race, language, homeland and origin, faith, or religious or political opinions, and disability. Until the 1980s, the GFCC gave these provisions a narrow scope when compared to protections conferred on other freedoms. Generally, the GFCC deploys a robust, three-step proportionality test when it adjudicates rights claims. When it came to Art. 3, however, the GFCC developed a more deferential level of scrutiny akin to what Americans would call 'rational basis' review. Under a full proportionality analysis, a court reviews an act or measure to ensure that (1) the means selected to achieve a purpose are 'suitable' to achieving that purpose (a suitability test); (2) the means chosen do not infringe upon the right more than is 'necessary' (a 'necessity' or least-restrictive means test); and (3) the cost of the measure – infringement on the right – is outweighed by the benefits of the measure under review (a residual 'balancing' test). The GFCC afforded the legislator wide discretion for making distinctions within categories falling under Arts. 3.2 and 3.3, in effect, stopping the analysis after step 1. Furthermore, the GFCC did not recognize indirect discrimination. With regard to sex equality, for example, the German constitution covered only discrimination that resulted from measures that overtly or intentionally treated men and women differently.

Abetted by German judges, the ECJ's equality case law fatally undermined the GFCC's position. German labour courts supplied the references to the ECJ in two foundational cases: *Bilka* (170/84) and *Rinner-Kühn* (C-171/88). These cases concerned the lawfulness of policies that denied part-time employees benefits afforded to full-time workers (pensions and sick-leave respectively), in situations in which women comprised the vast majority of the part-time labour force. In their references, German judges made it clear that they considered these practices, and the national statutes that permitted them, to be a form of indirect sex discrimination, and therefore unlawful under ex-Art. 119 EC. The ECJ responded by giving the referring courts what they wanted: a mandate to root out indirect discrimination in the workplace and in Germany's social policies. Further, because the right inheres in ex-Art. 119, the Court recognized its horizontal direct effect; employees could henceforth plead it directly against employers before national judges. As important, the ECJ insisted that judges use a full-blooded proportionality test to adjudicate such claims, whereas German judges would not be able to do so under the doctrines of the GFCC. In its final judgment in the *Bilka* saga (1986), the GFLC applied the ECJ's ruling to resolve the case.[12] The GFLC then began to invoke Art. 157 TFEU (ex-Art. 119 EC) as the source of the right, not the Basic Law, thereby marginalizing the GFCC.

The GFCC ruled on the case six years later, in 1992, pursuant to a constitutional complaint brought by the Bilka Department store, the loser in the case, attacking the GFLC's ruling as unconstitutional. The company claimed that the GFLC and the ECJ had struck the wrong balance, in that they undervalued the economic burdens to employers, while ignoring settled German constitutional case law. The GFCC rejected these arguments, in effect deferring to the ECJ.[13] In 1997, more than a decade after *Bilka* had been decided, the GFCC adopted the ECJ's framework as its own approach to indirect discrimination under Art. 3.2 of the Basic Law, citing the GFLC's and the ECJ's case law in the process.[14] In this episode, the ECJ and the German labour courts enhanced their status as rights-protecting courts, and they enhanced rights protection for German women. The GFCC, left behind and on the sidelines, changed its own rights jurisprudence in an effort to re-establish relevance.

With this background in mind, we turn to how age discrimination was addressed by German courts prior to the adjudication of the 2000 Framework Directive. German constitutional law does not expressly prohibit age discrimination. In the employment context, when the GFCC was asked to review the constitutionality of statutes that treated persons differently with reference to their age, it would review these provisions under Art. 12 Basic Law (freedom of occupation), treating Art. 3.1 as a supplementary, residual criterion. Only in cases not covered by Art. 12 or some other enumerated freedom, would the Court analyse a claim under the equality or non-discrimination heading (Art. 3 Basic Law) in a first stage. As noted above, this jurisprudence has consequences for the deference given by the GFCC to legislative authority. The GFCC applies proportionality analysis to most of the enumerated freedoms, but deploys a deferential, 'reasonableness' test to equality claims under Art. 3 Basic Law. In practical terms, this meant that the GFCC would almost never find a violation of the equality clause unless an enumerated freedom had also been violated. This case law has remained remarkably consistent since the late 1950s. The GFLC, on the other hand, had recognized an autonomous action for age discrimination in private contractual agreements since at least the 1980s.

In summary, when it came to protecting employees from discrimination, the GFLC's posture toward equality was open to EU law and flexible. Recall that it had embraced the horizontal direct effect of rights, before the GFCC sought to stifle that development in *Lüth*. Under its own jurisprudence, the GFLC continued to blend analysis under the General Clause and the Basic Law, balancing both against, say, the right to contract claimed by the employer. After *Bilka* and *Rinner-Kühn*, the GFLC could simply reference the ECJ's jurisprudence, while implicitly rejecting the GFCC's case law. Put differently, the ECJ's key rulings in the area strengthened what labour judges were already pre-disposed to do.[15] The GFCC, on the other hand, had painted itself into a doctrinal corner, making it appear insular and defensive. The 2000 Framework Directive would lay bare these tensions. Since the Directive prohibits, among other things, age discrimination in both its direct and indirect forms, and it applies to both the public and private sectors, the German legal order would be forced to adapt in deep, structural ways. The question was not if, but how, it would adapt.

4. THE *MANGOLD* CASE AND ITS IMPACT

In 2005, the ECJ issued its first ruling on the Framework Directive's provisions on age discrimination, pursuant to a reference sent by Judge Hauf, sitting on the Munich Labour Court of first instance. The case involved the employment of a lawyer, Mr Mangold, by another lawyer, Mr Held, to a fixed-term contract under conditions provided by federal statute governing part-time and fixed contract employment. The statute had been amended in 2003, to relax certain protections for employees, aged 52 and over, from dismissal. The alleged purpose of the statute was to facilitate the hiring of older workers. Mr Held had been an opponent of the 2003 amendment, on discrimination grounds, and had urged legislators to reject the amendment before the Bundestag. The proceedings established that Held had hired Mr Mangold for the express purpose of challenging the law in the courts,[16] but Judge Hauf set these objections aside, asserting authority to review the legality of the statute. Although the case raises a wide range of technical matters, we focus here on the major 'constitutional' issues.

Judge Hauf, whose antipathy for the statute was undisguised, faced several hurdles. Most important, the German statute under review had been amended prior to the deadline for transposing the Framework Directive into German law, and the government and the legislature were dragging their feet. EU directives, recall, are not possessed of horizontal direct effect. Further, the ECJ's doctrine of 'indirect effect', which requires judges to interpret national law with reference to EU law in order to make it effective, would only kick in once the transposition period had expired; and, in any event, age 52 was a rule that afforded no interpretive wiggle room. To make matters more complex, the German statute appeared to be compatible with the only pertinent EU legislation on the books, EU Directive 1999/70 on fixed-contract work, which does not address age discrimination.

In a wide-ranging reference, Judge Hauf sought to persuade the ECJ that the German statute was unlawful under EU law.[17] She began by pointing out that, in Germany, fixed-term-contract provisions had long been subject to constraints grounded in judicial precedent, including the rule that objective reasons must be given for limiting employment protection under such contracts, whereas the 2003 amendment did not require such justification when hiring workers aged 52 and over. Next, referencing the scholarly literature, which is far more contested than her portrayal would suggest,[18] Judge Hauf indicated that the German provisions probably violated the Framework Directive with respect to age discrimination. More important, she argued that the case was covered by EU fundamental rights, including provisions of the EU's Charter of Rights (then not in force): Art. 30 of the Charter announces a right to protection against unjustified dismissals; and Art. 21 prohibits age discrimination. Judge Hauf did not base her arguments on the Framework Directive, in part because the Directive had yet to be transposed into German law, and in part because she was seeking to constitutionalize the prohibition of age discrimination.

The ECJ, rejecting a more cautious approach urged by its Advocate-General, ruled that the question was governed by the general principle of equality, which included a right to non-discrimination on the basis of age. In framing the ruling in this way, the Court could circumvent the problem of horizontal direct effect, by basing its decision on fundamental rights,[19] not the Directive. Taking its cues from Judge Hauf, the Court held that the German provision under review discriminated against older employees, and that this harm could not be justified under the proportionality test required by Art. 6 of the Directive (which is itself based on the ECJ's equality jurisprudence). Because the national legislation fell within the scope of EU Law (through Directive 1999/70), the national judge is an agent of the EU legal order, authorized to 'provide all the criteria of interpretation needed ... to determine whether [national] rules are compatible with such a principle'. The ECJ then gave Judge Hauf what she wanted, authorization to enforce EU fundamental rights against the national rule under review.

The *Mangold* decision provoked a storm of protest.[20] Most notably, the former president of both the GFCC and the Federal Republic, Roman Herzog, attacked the Court in a public, frontal assault. In 2008, Herzog and his colleague, Lüder Gerken, published an article in the *Frankfurter Allgemeine Zeitung* entitled: 'Stoppt den Europäischen Gerichtshof' (Stop the ECJ). The Court's move to general principles was characterized as an *ultra vires* act under the criteria laid down by the GFCC in its famous ruling on the Maastricht Treaty.[21] In addition, the authors claimed that *Mangold* violated the constitutional rights of German employers (freedom of contract, freedom of occupation and the constitutional principle of legal certainty).

In the meantime, the GFLC quickly embraced the new jurisprudence in *Honeywell*, a case decided six months after the ECJ's *Mangold* ruling.[22] The facts were similar to those in *Mangold*, leading the GFLC to refuse to apply the relevant German provisions. The GFLC also took it upon itself to address the question of whether *Mangold* was *ultra vires* under the German Basic Law, rejecting the claim on multiple grounds. In doing so, the GFLC had conferred upon itself what arguably are inherently constitutional functions only to be exercised by the GFCC.

The GFCC ruled on the case four years later, pursuant to an individual complaint brought by the Honeywell Corporation. Observers considered the case to be a test of the GFCC's asserted authority to review the *ultra vires* nature of EU acts under its *Maastricht* ruling. A coalition of law professors from diverse backgrounds published an expert opinion attacking *Mangold*, and urging the GFCC to declare the ECJ's ruling *ultra vires* (Gerken *et al.* 2009). The GFCC dismissed these arguments,[23] over the dissent of one justice, thereby avoiding open conflict with the GFLC and the ECJ.

In our view, the GFCC had little to gain and much to lose in declaring the ECJ's *Mangold* decision invalid under German law. By the time of the GFCC's ruling (2010), the EU Charter of Rights had entered into force, changing at least the symbolic politics of the matter. In addition, the *Mangold* ruling had generated a wave of references from the German courts to the ECJ, interactions which the GFCC could not directly control. Last, to declare the ECJ's *Mangold* ruling *ultra vires* would be to admit an uncomfortable truth, namely that German standards for protecting fundamental rights were lower than European standards. The GFCC would then be faced with the difficult task of forcing the labour courts, which would be strongly supported by the ECJ, to comply with its ruling.

The ECJ, for its part, appeared to wobble. In its first post-*Mangold* case on the issue, *Palacios de la Villa* (C-411/05), Advocate-General Mazák forcefully criticized the *Mangold* ruling, characterizing it as a flight of fancy. The ECJ found the Spanish law under scrutiny to be justified under the Framework Directive, eschewing fundamental rights analysis under the general principles.

In the very next case, *Bartsch* (C-427/06), brought by the German GFLC, the Court held that the scope of the equality principle, with respect to age discrimination, did not extend to cases that have no connection to EU Law. *Bartsch* is also of interest in that it produced an opinion by Advocate-General Sharpston, elaborating ideas that could have significant influence on future developments. Sharpston advanced an expansive version of the *Mangold* doctrine, suggesting that the content of the general principle of non-discrimination would necessarily change over time, as society changes. The Court should be prepared to recognize new forms of discrimination, and seek to combat them on fundamental rights grounds, *Mangold* being just one instance in this unfolding process.

In 2010, the ECJ appeared to follow Sharpston's lead. In *Kücükdeveci* (C-555/07), the Higher Labour Court of Düsseldorf asked the ECJ to review the compatibility of a German Civil Code provision with EU law on age discrimination. Ms Kücükdeveci was employed from the age of 18 by Swedex, a company that dismissed her after 10 years of service. In calculating the period of notice owed to Ms Kücükdeveci, Swedex relied on a provision of the German Civil Code that allowed employers to exclude from consideration periods of work prior to an employee's 25th birthday. The plaintiff challenged the terms of her dismissal before a German labour court, which dismissed the claim. She appealed on the grounds that the provisions in question constituted age discrimination, in that she was not credited with work-time corresponding to her length of service. Labour courts operating in different Länder had produced contrary rulings on these same Civil Code provisions.[24]

The Düsseldorf court's reference to the ECJ expressed discomfort with the situation. The referral pointed out that, under the German Basic Law, it was bound by German statutes, and that only the GFCC possessed the authority to invalidate a German law. It then baldly stated that, given the GFCC's jurisprudence, a reference to the GFCC would be unlikely to help Ms Kücükdeveci; indeed, the referral cited two GFCC decisions upholding the provision in question in related cases. Nonetheless, the judges made it clear that they believed that the part of the Civil Code under review violated the EU's age discrimination principle, and could not be justified under the EU's Framework Directive. The referring judge then raised a major constitutional question: could any national court set aside a national norm if it considers that norm to be contrary to the principle of non-discrimination, or must the national judge be pre-authorized by the ECJ to do so?[25]

Six member state governments (the Czech Republic, Denmark, Germany, Ireland, the Netherlands and the United Kingdom) filed briefs or weighed in at oral argument, an unusually high number. On the major issues, the governments spoke in one voice: they opposed the *Mangold* doctrine; they objected to the horizontal direct effect of the principle of non-discrimination; and they rejected the notion that national courts could, on their own, set aside national norms, under *Mangold*. The Commission urged the Court to stay the course and confirm *Mangold*.

Ms Kücükdeveci won the case. The Court, while mentioning Art. 21 of the Charter (prohibiting age discrimination) strongly confirmed *Mangold*, which it relied on for the proposition that the 'general principles of EU law prohibits all discrimination on grounds of age, as given expression in Directive 2000/78.' The Court found the relevant provision of the Civil Code, dating from 1926, to be discriminatory and disproportionate, and ordered the referring judge to set it aside. It answered the key constitutional question as follows:

> It is for the national court, hearing proceedings between individuals, to ensure that the principle of non-discrimination on grounds of age, as given expression in Directive 2000/78, is complied with, disapplying if need be any contrary provision of national legislation, independently of whether it makes use of its entitlement . . . to ask the Court of Justice of the European Union for a preliminary ruling on the interpretation of that principle.

In an unusual move, the Higher Labour Court then issued a final judgement, setting aside the offending norms, and giving reasons for its decisions,[26] a mode meant to signal the advent of new precedent. The episode reveals constitutional pluralism in action.

Legislation transposing the Framework Act into German law entered into force in 2006. German courts have subsequently sent a wave of references to the ECJ, and these interactions will shape how the German statute will be implemented. Thus, the developments we have described comprise only the opening stages – in but one member state – of a long process of institutionalizing EU non-discrimination law through adjudication.

5. CONCLUSION

As this contribution has shown, the German labour courts willingly perform their roles as agents of the EU legal order, thereby enhancing the authority of the ECJ. They have also shown themselves to be more anxious to secure their own status as rights-protecting courts than to defend the autonomy of the German constitutional order. As it had done previously in the area of sex equality, the GFLC succeeded in marginalizing the GFCC, leaving the GFCC to play catch-up. The age of rights-based, constitutional pluralism in Europe is clearly upon us.[27]

Looking ahead, the ECJ's approach to non-discrimination raises a number of important questions. A first concerns the relationship between the Court's fundamental rights jurisprudence and the Charter of Rights. Under the Charter, which entered into force on 1 December 2009 (pursuant to the Lisbon Treaty), lawyers and judges will generate more rights-oriented litigation and preliminary references, and they will plead and decide cases differently. The ECJ, for its part, will be able to find rights issues implied in most cases it looks for them. Thus, there is every reason to expect that rights preoccupations will gradually come to dominate the Court's activities. Nonetheless, under Article 51(1) Charter, Charter rights apply to the member states 'only when they are implementing Union law', whereas the fundamental rights (as general principles) apply to the member states whenever they act 'within the scope of EU law'. Arguably, the latter comprises a broader mandate for judicial review. It is possible that the Court chose its formulation in *Mangold* in anticipation of the Charter's eventual promulgation, which would provide it with more reach and flexibility when dealing with references from the national courts. Today, there is hardly any area of national labour law, for example, that does not have a significant connection to EU law, and thus it is EU (not national-constitutional) rights that control. The German labour courts, we expect, will now aggressively work to construct the Charter for their own purposes.

In the meantime, litigation under the suite of directives on equality and non-discrimination, adopted since 2000 (Bell 2011), is exploding. In *Coleman* (C-303/06), a case involving equality for the disabled, the UK argued (as other states have) that the Framework Directive on Employment Equality lays down only 'minimum standards'. In his opinion, Advocate-General Maduro rejected this argument, but only after developing an expansive notion of equality and non-discrimination linked to the 'underlying values' of 'dignity and personal autonomy'. Under this conception, 'subtle' forms of indirect discrimination must also be covered. Maduro's formulation in *Coleman* fits well with the view of Advocate-General Sharpston (in *Bartsch*, discussed above) to the effect that the principle of non-discrimination is inherently expansive and adaptable to changing circumstances. The ECJ sided with Ms Coleman against the United Kingdom. If adjudicating non-discrimination claims in the EU means judicial recognition and enforcement of the underlying values of equality, then *Mangold* is only a modest but crucial step down the long path of judicialization through the protection of individual rights.

Biographical notes: Alec Stone Sweet is the Leitner Professor of Law, Politics, and International Studies, Yale Law School, Yale University. Kathleen Stranz is Ph.D. Candidate, Law Faculty, Leibniz University of Hannover, Germany.

NOTES

1 For a recent review of the social science literature on these topics, see Stone Sweet (2010).

2 In many European legal orders, three such sources – national constitutional rights, EU fundamental rights, the EU Charter of Rights, and the European Convention on Human Rights– co-exist and, in some areas, substantively overlap. Individuals have a choice of which source to plead; and judges have a choice of which right to enforce.

3 We take no normative view in this article on whether the constitutional rhetoric is appropriate, or whether developments in this domain of law are normatively defensible.

4 *Marshall I* (152/84); *Dori* (C-91/92). This gap in protection was partly closed by the emergence of the doctrine of *state liability*, holding that national judges can order state officials to compensate private parties for compliance failures; see *Francovich* (C-6 & 9/90); *Brasserie du Pecheur* (C-46/93 and C-48/93).

5 *Jenkins* (96/80); *Bilka* (170/84); *Rinner- Kühn* (171/88); as consolidated in *Enderby* (C-127/92).

6 The lone exception being the United Kingdom.

7 On constitutional pluralism more generally, see Stone Sweet (2009).

8 Bundesarbeitsgericht [1954], BAGE 1, 185.

9 Bundesarbeitsgericht [1957], BAGE 4, 274.

10 Bundesverfassungsgericht [1958], BVerfGE 7, 198.

11 Bundesarbeitsgericht [1956], BAGE 3, 180.

12 Bundesarbeitsgericht [1986], BAGE 53, 161. Körner (2001: 1046) notes that the GFLC went further than the ECJ, making justification of discriminatory effects more difficult for employers.

13 Bundesverfassungsgericht [1992], *Neue Zeitschrift für Arbeitsrecht* 10(5): 213–15.

14 Bundesverfassungsgericht [1997], BVerfGE 97, 35.

15 More generally, German labour law has always been regulated through a style of relatively autonomous judicial law-making that resembles practices found in the common law, as well as in ECJ decision-making, which has facilitated these dialogues. We thank an anonymous reviewer for emphasizing this important point.

16 This fact scandalized specialists, including Bauer (2005).

17 Arbeitsgericht München 2004, *Neue Zeitschrift für Arbeitsrecht-Rechtsprechungsreport* 10(1): 43–47.

18 Däubler (2001) argued that the provision violated the Directive, while Koberski (2005) disagreed.

19 The Court derived the right from 'various international instruments and ... the constitutional traditions common to the Member States'.

20 Including Bauer and Arnold (2006), Hailbronner (2008) and Preis (2006).

21 Bundesverfassungsgericht [1993], BVerfGE 89, 155. In that ruling, the GFCC warned that it would invalidate any EU act having the effect of depriving German legislative organs of their control over legal norms created at the EU level. Private parties thereby possessed the right to plead the *ultra vires* nature of Community acts before all German judges, and to bring constitutional complaints alleging the same to the GFCC.

22 Bundesarbeitsgericht [2006], BAGE 118, 76.

23 Bundesverfassungsgericht [2010], BVerfGE 126, 286. English translation available online at: www.bundesverfassungsgericht.de/entscheidungen/rs20100706_2bvr2661 06en.html (accessed 7 September 2011).

24 Landesarbeitsgericht Berlin-Brandenburg [2007] found a violation of EU law, *Neue Zeitschrift für Arbeitsrecht-Rechtsprechungsreport* 13(1): 17–19, whereas Arbeitsgericht Lörrach [2007] did not, *Arbeit und Recht* 3: 184.

25 From the perspective of the ECJ's case law on supremacy, the question is a version of one that has already been decided; see *Simmenthal II* (106/77). The member states only formally accepted the ECJ's doctrine of supremacy in 2007, in Declaration 17 'Concerning Primacy'. *Declarations Annexed to the Final Act of the Intergovernmental Conference which Adopted the Treaty of Lisbon*, available online at: http://eur-lex.europa.eu/LexUriServ/LexUriServ.do?uri=OJ:C:2008:115:0335:0359:EN:PDF (accessed 7 September 2011).

26 Landesarbeitsgericht Düsseldorf [2010], *Zeitschrift für Wirtschaftsrecht* 31(12): 596.

27 The evolution of the European Convention on Human Rights, as a body of directly effective, supra-legislative (if infra-constitutional) rights, has also generated dynamics that are rapidly consolidating constitutional pluralism as a general, structural feature of European law (Keller and Stone Sweet 2008: 682–89).

REFERENCES

Alter, K. (2001) *Establishing the Supremacy of European Law*, Oxford: Oxford University Press.

Bauer, J.-H. (2005) 'Ein Stück aus dem Tollhaus: Altersbefristung und der EuGH', *Neue Zeitschrift für Arbeitsrecht* 22(14): 800–3.

Bauer, J.-H. and Arnold, C. (2006) 'Auf „Junk" folgt „Mangold" – Europarecht verdrängt deutsches Arbeitsrecht', *Neue Juristische Wochenzeitschrift* 59(1): 6–12.

Bell, M. (2011) 'The principle of equal treatment: widening and deepening', in P. Craig and G. De Burca (eds), *The Evolution of EU Law*, Oxford: Oxford University Press, pp. 611–86.

Böhm, M. (2008) 'Umfang und Grenzen eines europäischen Verbots der Altersdiskriminierung im deutschen Recht', *Juristenzeitung* 63(7): 324–30.

Cichowski, R. (2001) 'Judicial rulemaking and the institutionalization of EU sex equality policy', in A. Stone Sweet *et al.* (eds), *The Institutionalization of Europe*, Oxford: Oxford University Press, pp. 113–36.

Cichowski, R. (2007) *The European Court and Civil Society: Litigation, Mobilization and Governance*, Cambridge: Cambridge University Press.

Däubler, W. (2001) 'Das neue Teilzeit- und Befristungsgesetz', *Zeitschrift für Wirtschaftsrecht* 22(6): 217–25.

Ellis, E. (1998) *European Community Sex Equality Law*, Oxford: Oxford University Press.

Ellis, E. (2005) *EU Anti-Discrimination Law*, Oxford: Oxford University Press.

Fuchsloch, C. (1995) *Das Verbot der mittelbaren Geschlechtsdiskriminierung*, Baden-Baden: Nomos.

Gerken, L., Rieble, V., Roth, G.H., Stein, T. and Streinz, R. (2009) *Mangold als ausbrechender Rechtsakt*, München: Sellier.

Hailbronner, K. (2006) 'Hat der EuGH eine Normverwerfungskompetenz?', *Neue Zeitschrift für Arbeitsrecht* 23(15): 811–16.

Herzog, R. and Gerken, L. (2008) 'Stoppt den Europäischen Gerichtshof', *Frankfurter Allgemeine Zeitung*, 8 September.

Kelemen, R.D. (2011) *Eurolegalism: The Transformation of Law and Regulation in the European Union*, Cambridge, MA: Harvard University Press.

Kelemen, R.D. and Schmidt, S.K. (2012) 'Introduction – the European Court of Justice and legal integration: perpetual momentum?', *Journal of European Public Policy* 19(1): 1–7.

Keller, H. and Stone Sweet, A. (eds) (2008) *A Europe of Rights: The Impact of the European Convention on Human Rights on National Legal Systems*, Oxford: Oxford University Press.

Koberski, W. (2005) 'Befristete Arbeitsverträge älterer Arbeitnehmer im Einklang mit Gemeinschaftsrecht', *Neue Zeitschrift für Arbeitsrecht* 22(2): 79–84.

Kokott, J. (1995) 'Die Gleichstellung von Mann und Frau – Deutsches Verfassungsrecht und europäisches Gemeinschaftsrecht', *Neue Juristische Wochenschrift* 48(16): 1049–57.

Körner, M. (2001) 'Der Dialog des EuGH mit den deutschen Arbeitsgerichten', *Neue Zeitschrift für Arbeitsrecht* 18(19): 1046–54.

Lenaerts, K. (1990) 'Constitutionalism and the many faces of federalism', *American Journal of Comparative Law* 38(2): 205–63.

Mancini, F. (1989) 'The making of a constitution for Europe', *Common Market Law Review* 26(4): 595–614.
Mattli, W. and Slaughter, A.-M. (1998) 'Revisiting the European Court of Justice', *International Organization* 52(1): 177–209.
Nyikos, S. (2003) 'The preliminary reference process: national court implementation, changing opportunity structures and litigant desistment', *European Union Politics* 4(4): 397–419.
Panke, D. (2007) 'The European Court of Justice as an agent of Europeanization: restoring compliance with EU law', *Journal of European Public Policy* 14(6): 847–66.
Prechal, S. (1995) *Directives in European Law*, Oxford: Oxford University Press.
Preis, U. (2006) 'Das Verbot der Altersdiskriminierung als Gemeinschaftsgrundrecht – Der Fall Mangold und die Folgen', *Neue Zeitschrift für Arbeitsrecht* 23(8): 401–10.
Quint, P.E. (1989) 'Free speech and private law in German constitutional theory', *Maryland Law Review* 48(2): 247–347.
Schmidt, S.K. (2012) 'Who cares about nationality? The path-dependent case law of the ECJ from goods to citizens', *Journal of European Public Policy* 19(1): 8–24.
Stone Sweet, A. (2004) *The Judicial Construction of Europe*, Oxford: Oxford University Press.
Stone Sweet, A. (2009) 'Constitutionalism, legal pluralism, and international regimes', *Indiana Journal of Global Legal Studies* 16(2): 621–45.
Stone Sweet, A. (2010) 'The European Court of Justice and the judicialization of EU governance', *Living Reviews in EU Governance*, available online at http://europeangovernance.livingreviews.org/ (accessed 7 September 2011).
Stone Sweet, A. and Mathews, J. (2008) 'Proportionality balancing and global constitutionalism', *Columbia Journal of Transnational Law* 47(1): 73–165.
Weiler, J. (1991) 'The transformation of Europe', *Yale Law Journal* 100(8): 2403–83.

With Luxembourg in mind . . . the remaking of national policies in the face of ECJ jurisprudence

Michael Blauberger

ABSTRACT This article analyses EU member state political responses to ECJ challenges. Faced with high consensus requirements at the European level, member states often have to respond unilaterally and explore how to pursue autonomous regulatory goals in 'EU-compatible' ways. Member states' domestic responses to one prominent series of ECJ judgments (*Laval, Rüffert, Commission vs Luxembourg*) are traced from a Europeanization perspective. The case studies show that, by forging a consensus which includes potential litigants and by building on existing legal precedent, member state governments can preserve significant parts of their original legislation while making it ECJ-proof.

INTRODUCTION

When the European Court of Justice (ECJ) delivered its preliminary ruling on the *Laval* case (C-341/05) in December 2007, critical comments on the EU's judiciary reached an extraordinary level. The ECJ was accused of promoting 'social dumping' and launching an 'attack on workers' rights' (cf. Mayer 2009: 8). Owing to the ECJ's expansive interpretation of European market freedoms, it was argued, the 'very autonomy of Member States' labour and social constitutions is undermined' (Joerges and Rödl 2009: 13). As a response, commentators considered the 'nuclear option' of member states' deliberate non-compliance with European jurisprudence (Scharpf 2009b: 200).

Certainly, balancing community and autonomy has become more delicate for the ECJ in an enlarged and deeply integrated European Union (EU). Yet, the nuclear option of outright resistance against ECJ rulings has not been raised or used as a threat by member state governments. At the same time, joint responses to correct the European judiciary are faced with the high consensus requirements of EU decision-making. Consequently, challenged by ECJ jurisprudence, member state governments are typically left with one immediate response: they may explore unilaterally how to preserve domestic regulatory goals in a way that is compatible with the requirements of the European judiciary.

Thus, in response to the ECJ's preliminary ruling in the *Laval* case, the Swedish government inquired about possible legislative action:

> The objective must be to maintain the fundamental principle in the Swedish labour market: that the main responsibility for regulating pay and employment terms and conditions has been assigned to the social partners. At the same time, Community law ... must also be fully respected. (Swedish Government 2008: 8)

This contribution investigates *why* and *how* member state governments regulate 'with Luxembourg in mind', i.e., bringing national legislation in conformity with ECJ case law while trying to preserve domestic regulatory autonomy as much as possible. The next section locates the study within the literature on judicialization. The third section develops an analytical framework to study the underlying interests and the strategies of member state governments for making domestic regulation ECJ-proof. On this basis, the fourth section analyses EU member states' legislative responses to a series of three closely interrelated ECJ judgments: *Laval*, *Rüffert* (C-346/06), and *Commission vs Luxembourg* (C-319/06). In contrast to the harsh initial reactions, the text concludes that EU member states have been able to preserve their original regulatory goals in EU-compatible ways, albeit to varying degrees and through different strategies.

POLITICAL RESPONSES TO EUROPEAN JURISPRUDENCE

EU judicial politics has attracted increasing attention from scholars of European integration during the past decade. The debate has moved beyond the intergovernmentalism vs neofunctionalism divide and specified mechanisms and scope conditions of European integration through law. The close linkage of national and European courts through preliminary reference procedures, the differing time horizons of judges and politicians, the self-sustaining nature of legal discourse and precedent, and the role of private litigation have been put forward to account for the strength of the European judiciary (Stone Sweet 2010). As a result, the ECJ decides not only individual cases of conflict, but influences more broadly the strategic behaviour of political actors.

Most studies on this 'judicialization of politics' focus at the EU level (see Stone Sweet 2010: 27f.). For example, the European Commission has been shown to instrumentalize the threat of court activism to overcome member state resistance against European legislation (Schmidt 2000). In principle, member states may respond collectively to European jurisprudence by further harmonizing EU policies or by turning back court-driven integration through re-nationalizing policies. In both directions, however, member states face high consensus hurdles. Whereas the latter option of overriding the ECJ has proven to be largely hypothetical (Stone Sweet and Brunell 2010), positive integration often lags behind and can only partially compensate for court-driven negative integration (Scharpf 2009a: 6f.).

At least in the short run, therefore, EU member states can only respond to ECJ challenges at the national level. Domestic responses to European jurisprudence are often difficult to detect and the common dichotomy of 'compliance' vs 'non-compliance' hardly captures the whole spectrum of possible responses. Outright non-compliance with ECJ rulings constitutes one extreme. On the opposite side, 'regulatory surrender' denotes a situation in which domestic action is fully determined or even pre-empted by the Court's jurisprudence. In between these extremes, however, there normally exists a grey area in which member state governments may explore how to preserve autonomous domestic regulation in EU-compatible ways (see Figure 1).

Most prominently, Lisa Conant has investigated this grey area and argued that EU member states typically 'contain' compliance by applying ECJ rulings only to the immediate court cases while neglecting their broader policy implications (Conant 2002: 32). The following analysis builds on and extends beyond Conant's argument in at least two regards.

Firstly, broader policy reform 'with Luxembourg in mind' may be enacted precisely to contain the domestic impact of ECJ jurisprudence. By contrast, restricting the enforcement of ECJ rulings to individual cases entails the risk of further Court challenges and the resulting legal uncertainty is highly undesirable for domestic policy-makers (Schmidt *et al.* 2008). Accordingly, various recent policy studies found that the ECJ triggers broader reforms at the national level, even in areas where no genuine EU policy exists, e.g., regarding corporate taxation (Genschel and Jachtenfuchs 2011) and healthcare policy (Martinsen and Vrangbæk 2008).

Secondly, containing the domestic impact of ECJ jurisprudence does not necessarily contradict full compliance with EU law. Court rulings hardly ever prescribe a specific policy response, but rather circumscribe a legal corridor within which member states can remake their policies in various EU-compatible ways. Thus, even full compliance with an ECJ ruling may at least partly be reconciled with the preservation of autonomous domestic regulation. The following section proposes an analytical framework to assess empirically if and

	←Less integration		**More integration →**
EU level	Re-nationalization		Harmonization
National level	Non-compliance	EU-compatible re-regulation	Regulatory surrender

Figure 1 Political responses to European jurisprudence

through which strategies member state governments manage to defend regulatory autonomy in EU-compatible ways.

REGULATING WITH LUXEMBOURG IN MIND

Two aspects need to be addressed separately in order to analyse *why* and *how* EU member state governments regulate 'with Luxembourg in mind': The next subsection discusses when member state governments actually have an *interest* in regulating 'with Luxembourg in mind'. Subsequently, two types of *strategies* to arrive at EU-compatible domestic regulation are distinguished.

Balancing community and autonomy

Why do EU member state governments re-regulate 'with Luxembourg in mind' rather than disregard the Court or abandon domestic regulation? If they are faced with *strong conflicting pressures to adjust and to preserve domestic regulation*, national policy-makers have to strike a delicate balance between community and autonomy. Europeanization research is mostly concerned with the implementation of EU policies (Töller 2010: 429), but it can also help to understand these balancing processes in the context of the judicialization of domestic policy-making.

On the one hand, in order to expect any domestic response to an EU impulse, there has to be, first, some latent misfit (or 'mismatch', cf. Héritier [2001: 9]) between existing European and national law and, second, there have to be interested actors who actually transform this misfit into adjustment pressures (Börzel and Risse 2007: 490f.). An ECJ ruling which finds national rules incompatible with European law identifies a misfit, but it is hardly sufficient to promote domestic change single-handedly (Conant 2002: 15; Slagter 2009: 190). In addition, interested actors need to take up the ECJ's case law and supply or threaten to supply further legal challenges in the case of domestic inaction. The main actors who bring cases to the Court are the European Commission (through infringement proceedings) and private litigants (through preliminary references from national courts). Compliance research shows that most infringement proceedings get closed at an early stage and member states normally yield to the Commission's arguments (Börzel 2003: 217). Furthermore, as an alternative or complement to the Commission's limited enforcement capacities, decentralized private litigation has become increasingly important over time (Kelemen 2011: 28, 88).

On the other hand, European impulses often meet with strong resistance at the domestic level. Existing research points to the adjustment costs for political actors, in particular veto players, and to the lack of resonance with domestic political culture as major factors inhibiting Europeanization (Börzel and Risse 2007: 492f.). Sometimes, ECJ rulings may provide a welcome opportunity to overcome this resistance, e.g., when they help incumbent member state governments to further their own agenda (Treib 2003) and to shift the blame for unpopular decisions to the EU level (Tallberg 2002: 27). Yet, if their own constituency has a strong interest in preserving the regulatory status quo and is negatively affected by an ECJ ruling, or if the Court's jurisprudence clashes with the domestic political culture at large, member state governments face a dilemma: regulatory surrender is not an option, neither is outright non-compliance and, hence, they have to explore how to revise domestic regulation in an EU-compatible way.

In sum, ECJ judgments do not trigger an automatic response at the national level. Interests matter, both to turn a particular misfit identified by the Court into adjustment pressures and to counter these pressures in order to preserve autonomous national regulation.

Strategies of ECJ-proof regulation

But *how* can EU member state governments re-regulate 'with Luxembourg in mind'? Above all, in order to make national legislation ECJ-proof, policy-makers need to be creative. A great diversity of possible strategies to arrive at EU-compatible regulation exists: for example, member states may go for an informal approval of draft legislation by the European Commission or they may promote private self-regulation instead of formal legislation in order to avoid legal conflicts at the EU level (Töller 2004: 10–13). Two regulatory strategies are particularly pertinent for the subsequent empirical analysis and, therefore, deserve a more detailed discussion regarding their conditions for success.

First, the *inclusion of potential litigants* can help to forge a regulatory consensus which does not get challenged in court. Hence, to prevent preliminary references from domestic courts, national policy-makers can involve private parties in rule-making and mitigate conflicts about rule application before they escalate in court. Moreover, informal contacts to Brussels may help to anticipate potential infringement action on the part of the European Commission. The success of this inclusion strategy depends on the degree of *political consensus* or *dissent* among the relevant actors. If a regulatory solution is supported by a strong societal consensus, preliminary references by national courts become less likely. For example, Marlene Wind (2010: 1059) explains the reluctance of Swedish and Danish courts to refer cases to the ECJ by consensual and corporatist features of national policy-making: 'The Nordic states are unitary states, extremely homogeneous and have a corporatist structure. Conflicts are therefore usually resolved outside the court system.' By contrast, if the Commission is split regarding the EU-compatibility of a national measure, the likelihood of an infringement proceeding decreases. Decisions are taken by the Commission as a collective body (i.e., *de jure* by an absolute majority and *de facto* mostly consensual). Compliance research hints at the Commission's selectiveness in pursuing possible infringements (Hartlapp and Falkner 2009: 292). As a consequence, internal dissent in the Commission may raise member states' chances of finding support at the EU level and of avoiding infringement action.

A second strategy to regulate 'with Luxembourg in mind' is the *emulation of EU-compatible rules* from other member states. Emulation reduces the costs of designing EU-compatible rules oneself and the uncertainty about possible legal challenges. In addition, the existence of EU-compatible rules elsewhere also empowers the proponents of re-regulation against the argument that domestic action is pre-empted by the Court's jurisprudence. The success of this emulation strategy depends on the *availability of legal precedent* broadly understood. If the ECJ has already explicitly endorsed national regulation in one case, other member states can use this template for designing their own policies ECJ-proof. Less formal, if the Commission negotiates a compromise with one member state government and refrains from infringement action, this compromise may become a model for other countries. Finally, if national regulation is considered EU-compatible among legal scholars and it has survived uncontested for some time, this provides no guarantee for the future, but nevertheless it might suffice to serve as an example for others. The following empirical analysis discusses these strategies in practice.

NATIONAL RESPONSES TO THE POSTED WORKERS CASES

The remainder of this text traces national responses to a series of closely interrelated ECJ judgments: *Laval*; *Rüffert*; and *Commission vs Luxembourg*. The cases have been chosen for two main reasons. Given the extraordinary public attention they attracted, these judgments are 'most likely cases' to find member state governments under simultaneous pressures to adjust and to preserve national rules. At the same time, many observers have interpreted the judgments as severe restrictions of national regulatory autonomy (Joerges and Rödl 2009: 13; Malmberg and Sigeman 2008). They are, therefore, 'hard cases' concerning member states' chances of successfully preserving national autonomy in an EU-compatible way. Before tracing national responses from the immediate reception of the Court's judgments to the eventual legislative reform, the cases will be briefly presented.

Laval, Rüffert, Commission vs Luxembourg

The ECJ ruled on *Laval*, *Rüffert* and *Commission vs Luxembourg* in late 2007 and early 2008; the judgment in *Viking* (C-438/05)[1] is usually regarded as completing the ECJ's '*Laval* quartet' (Malmberg 2010: 8). The rulings challenged national measures to protect workers' rights in the context of EU enlargement. In *Laval*, *Rüffert* and *Commission vs Luxemburg*, national measures were found to restrict the European freedom of services under the Posted Workers Directive 96/71/EC (hereafter PWD). According to the PWD, the Court ruled, posted workers could not be subjected to the entire terms and conditions of work applicable in a member state, in particular if those conditions stemmed from non-universally applicable collective agreements, but only to a nucleus of mandatory rules for minimum protection.

The *Laval* conflict involved the Swedish building workers' union (*Byggnads*) and a Latvian construction company (*Laval un Partneri*) which had been commissioned to build a school in Sweden. After negotiations had failed between these two parties, Laval signed a collective agreement with a Latvian trade union instead. Swedish trade unionists denied the validity of this agreement and took collective action by blocking the construction site. Laval brought the conflict to the Swedish Labour Court which eventually referred the case to the ECJ. The ECJ acknowledged the fundamental right of trade unions to take collective action, but found the specific actions in this case, blocking the construction site, disproportionate. In addition, the Swedish '*Lex Britannia*' which permitted collective action irrespective of existing collective agreements under foreign law was found to be discriminatory.

The *Rüffert* judgment challenged the Public Procurement Act of the German *Land* Lower-Saxony. According to this act, construction firms could only win a public tender if they committed themselves by a 'collective agreements declaration' (*Tariftreueerklärung*, cf. Rödl 2009: 2) to pay at least the wages prescribed by the local collective agreement. A German company won a tender and subcontracted work to a Polish company. When it became public that Polish workers were paid less than their German colleagues at the site, the government annulled the contract and imposed financial penalties. The German company's complaint reached the ECJ as a preliminary reference. The Court ruled that Lower Saxony's Public Procurement Act imposed an unjustified restriction of the freedom to provide services under the PWD, in particular as it protected only workers in the public sector.

Finally, *Commission vs Luxembourg* resulted from an infringement proceeding of the European Commission which argued that Luxembourg's legislation went beyond what was allowed under the PWD. Referring to Article 3(10) of the PWD on public policy exceptions, Luxembourg had extended its entire regulation regarding terms and conditions of employment to situations of cross-border service provision. The ECJ followed the Commission's argument and declared that Luxembourg, by imposing requirements on foreign service providers that were not covered by a narrow interpretation of the public policy exception, e.g., rules on part-time and fixed-term work, had implemented the PWD incorrectly.

The ECJ judgments spurred controversial discussions at the European level, but action developed slowly. In a resolution of 22 October 2008 on 'Challenges to Collective Agreements in the EU', the European Parliament suggested a reform of the PWD. The same month, the Commission organized a 'Forum on Workers' Rights and Economic Freedoms' to consult member states and social partners on the consequences of the ECJ's rulings. A joint report of European social partners from March 2010 shows fundamental disagreement about the desirability of a reform of the PWD (European Social Partners 2010: 7, 14). In the run-up to his re-election in September 2009, Commission President Barroso proposed a new Regulation instead of revising the PWD; the idea was included in the Commission's communication 'Towards a Single Market Act' in November 2010 and a first legislative draft was announced for late 2011.

In the short and medium term, therefore, EU member states had to react domestically to the *Laval* jurisprudence. By the end of 2010, legislative responses to the three ECJ judgments were taken in four countries – those directly affected plus Denmark (Eurofound 2010: 24f.). These legislative responses will now be analysed in turn.

Laval: Swedish and Danish responses

The ECJ's judgment in *Laval* met with strong resistance not only in Sweden but also in Denmark. In both countries, posted work is regulated through collective agreements which are not declared universally applicable and not complemented by a statutory minimum wage. The 'Nordic model' of autonomous collective bargaining is usually considered an essential feature of the Swedish and Danish political systems (Malmberg and Sigeman 2008: 1117) and, hence, the goal of its preservation was not generally contested. Even Swedish Prime Minister Reinfeld, who had been openly critical of *Byggnads* in the *Laval* conflict before his liberal–conservative government came into office in 2006, eventually reaffirmed the 'non-partisan' roots of the Swedish model (Davesne 2009: 13; Woolfson *et al.* 2010: 341).

At the same time, the threat of continued private litigation after *Laval* created strong adjustment pressures in Sweden and Denmark. The Confederation of Swedish Enterprise (*Svenskt Näringsliv*) regarded the *Laval* conflict as an opportunity to curtail collective action rights and even provided financial support to the Latvian company before the Swedish Labour Court (Woolfson *et al.* 2010: 341). *Svenskt Näringsliv* welcomed the Court's ruling and called for quick legislative change. In Denmark, a similar case had emerged in 2005, but was not referred to the ECJ (Neergaard and Nielsen 2010: 458f.). The Danish Labour Court argued that it was sufficiently clear that collective action did not constitute an unjustified obstacle to European market freedoms. After *Laval*, however, when Danish trade unions continued to be involved in a considerable number of collective actions against foreign service providers, the Danish court could hardly have upheld the same argument.

Notably, the threat of further private litigation was not accompanied by an equal challenge from the European Commission. In Court, the Commission refrained from taking a pronounced position and after the ruling it mainly argued that it was for national authorities and social partners to come up with adequate responses (Malmberg 2010: 10). In fact, intra-Commission tensions became apparent. When the former Commissioner for Internal Market and Services McCreevy publicly criticized the Swedish government and unions during the conflict, President Barroso had to clarify that the Commission did not take sides (Lindstrom 2010: 1315).

The initial reactions of the Swedish and Danish governments were the same: given that joint European action was highly unlikely in the near future, commissions were appointed to propose domestic legislative adjustments in response to the ECJ's jurisprudence (Malmberg 2010: 10–14). Their mandate was to preserve as far as possible, the systems of autonomous collective bargaining in an EU-compatible way (Danish Ministry of Employment 2008: 3; Swedish Government 2008: 8). In both countries, social partners were centrally included in the process of legislative reform: as a reference group advising the Laval inquiry in Sweden and as direct members of the tripartite Laval commission in Denmark. In addition, the Swedish Laval inquiry also drew on informal contacts with other member states, including Denmark, and the European Commission (Swedish Government 2008: 3).

Owing to different levels of political consensus, however, this inclusion strategy did not work equally smoothly in Sweden and Denmark. Already during the *Laval* conflict, Swedish trade unions and employers had taken rather uncompromising positions (Davesne 2009: 12). The social partners in the reference group to the Swedish Laval inquiry could not reach a compromise by themselves and the final report, although written by the head of the Swedish Mediation Office, Claes Stråth, was not fully supported by either of the two sides.[2] By contrast, the Danish response was essentially based on a consensus among social partners to proactively protect autonomous collective bargaining and to 'crack the nuts ourselves' rather than undermining mutual trust by opportunistically bringing conflicts to the EU level (Bruun and Jonsson 2010: 22f.).

As a result, the Laval commissions concluded their work at different rates and legislative changes were adopted by the end of 2008 in Denmark and by the end of 2009 in Sweden. While the Danish Laval report comprises only 21 pages, the Swedish Laval inquiry covers more than 400 pages and engages in a detailed analysis of potential legal conflicts:

> The [Danish] idea seems to be to reach a national compromise which will not be challenged ... In Sweden it was clear early on that no such consensus would be reached ... If the Danish report seems anxious not to uncover any hidden obstacles for the compromise, the intention of the Swedish report seems to be to leave no stone unturned in finding a solution that could not be legally questioned. (Malmberg 2010: 14)

The commonalities and the specifics of the two reform processes are also reflected in the substance of Danish[3] and Swedish[4] legislative responses: most fundamentally, both reforms managed to preserve the autonomy of collective bargaining, rather than introducing a statutory minimum wage or declaring collective agreements generally binding (Rönnmar 2010: 285). While explicitly endorsing the latter options, the ECJ had conceded that member states were 'free to choose a system at the national level which is not expressly mentioned ... in that directive, provided that it does not hinder the provision of services between the Member States' (No. 68 of the *Laval* judgment). Based on this statement and on an 'innovative' re-interpretation of Article 3(8) of the PWD (Malmberg 2010: 12, 14), both reforms reaffirm the autonomy of collective bargaining, but introduce conditions for the exercise of collective action.

As a consequence, collective agreements can only be enforced through collective action against foreign service providers if they correspond to existing nationwide collective agreements and do not define conditions beyond the 'hard core' of the PWD.

A closer look at the legislative responses to *Laval*, also reveals significant differences. Broader consensus among social partners enabled Denmark to explore more boldly the limits of its remaining national regulatory autonomy. Danish legislation defines 'minimum pay' more widely than the Swedish reform (Kilpatrick 2009: 858; Malmberg 2010: 12f.). Conditions regarding holidays and leave that are imposed upon Danish employers may be 'converted' into a fixed sum when calculating the minimum pay demanded from foreign service providers. By contrast, the Swedish reform explicitly prohibits collective action if an employer can show that the posted workers enjoy at least as favourable conditions as follow from the minimum conditions of a collective agreement. This 'evidential requirement' can be met by the employer through a collective agreement in the home country or simply through personal employment contracts (Rönnmar 2010: 285).

In sum, Sweden and Denmark managed to contain the impact of ECJ jurisprudence and to re-make domestic legislation in EU-compatible ways. The Court's narrow interpretation of the PWD still allowed both countries to maintain their systems of autonomous collective bargaining. In practice, the reforms only affect collective bargaining when posted workers are involved, and even then most foreign service providers still voluntarily agree with traditional collective agreements, both in Denmark and in Sweden.[5] In critical cases, the new legislation obliges trade unions to limit their claims and make them more transparent if they want to legally take collective action. In cases of high legal uncertainty, they may opt to refrain from collective action in order to avoid court challenges. Despite this 'chilling effect' (Rönnmar 2010: 286) on trade unions, collective action against foreign (and domestic) service providers is still taken quite regularly and so far the EU-compatibility of the new rules has not been challenged. The inclusion of social partners, thus, was crucial for the Swedish and Danish governments to revise their legislation on posted workers 'with Luxembourg in mind'; infringement action by the Commission was not perceived as imminent. In the face of heavy political contestation, Sweden pursued a more cautious and legalistic reform, while Denmark could build on a stronger societal consensus and explore its remaining regulatory autonomy more boldly.

Rüffert*: varying responses of German *Länder

The *Rüffert* case marked the climax of a political and legal battle about the protection of labour standards in public procurement which had been fought for years in Germany (Rödl 2009: 3–6). Owing to the failure to agree on a federal law on collective agreement declarations, various *Länder* introduced corresponding provisions into their public procurement law; governments led by

Social Democrats (SPD) as well as by Conservatives (CDU/CSU). As a result of this previous history, both major parties were under significant pressure to preserve autonomous regulation after *Rüffert.*

At the same time, *Länder* governments could not simply ignore the judgment: the ruling strongly re-affirmed the ECJ's reasoning in *Laval* and there were explicit threats of private litigation in the case of non-compliance which could have even involved damages claims. Besides private litigation, the Commission also took a pronounced position which was largely congruent with the Court's final ruling and, hence, legislative inaction would most likely lead to infringement procedures. For the Liberals (FDP), which had opposed collective agreement declarations already before *Rüffert*, the risk of new litigation offered an opportunity to require their adjustment or abolishment.

As an immediate response to *Rüffert*, all German *Länder* with similar legislation as Lower-Saxony disapplied the contested provisions in April and May 2008. Yet, after overcoming the '*Rüffert* shock' (Schulten 2010a), several *Länder* revised their legislation in order to defend at least partly the original idea of the declarations while making it EU-compatible (see Table 1).

In contrast to the Swedish and Danish cases, re-regulating EU-compatible was not as widely accepted as a political goal in the first place, but positions varied between governing parties according to their main constituencies' interests (cf. Sack 2010). As a consequence, *Länder* governed by centre–right coalitions (CDU/CSU, FDP) largely abolished the contested provisions and did not engage in re-regulation. Lower-Saxony seems an exception among centre–right governments, but it kept only a very restricted and largely symbolic reference to collective agreement declarations. Governing coalitions which cannot be clearly classified as centre–right or centre–left reacted in a mixed way. Their reactions basically reflect the internal divide of the CDU/CSU on the issue of collective agreement declarations (Rödl 2009: 6). Labour and unions may not be the core constituency of the conservative party, but their interests can hardly be ignored either. Finally, all governments led by the social-democrat party (SPD) reformed or are still reforming their public procurement legislation so as to include the requirement of collective agreement declarations and other social criteria.

To revise their public procurement legislation in EU-compatible ways, *Länder* governments relied on extensive legal expertise and on emerging precedent. The earliest reforms after *Rüffert* could not draw on any existing model, but had to enter unknown legal territory. Thus, Bremen commissioned two legal surveys (Hänlein *et al.* 2008: 30) before adopting new legislation, including among other things a specific minimum wage for public procurement. To avoid any conflict about its EU-compatibility, however, the minimum wage is not applied to public tenders beyond the relevant thresholds of European procurement law. The government of Berlin wanted to go further and commissioned another three legal surveys (Rödl 2011). All of them confirmed the possibility of designing an EU-compatible minimum wage for public

Table 1 Collective agreement declarations after *Rüffert* (as at 31 December 2010)

Land	*Gov. parties*	*Collective agreement declarations*	*Min. wage*	*Date of revision*
Centre–right governments				
Baden-Württemberg	CDU, FDP	No	–	–
Bavaria	CSU, FDP	No (abolished after Rüffert)	–	04/2008
Hesse	CDU, FDP	No (disapplied after Rüffert)	–	04/2008
Lower-Saxony	CDU, FDP	Yes	–	12/2008
Saxony	CDU, FDP	No	–	–
Schleswig-Holstein	CDU, FDP	No (disapplied after Rüffert)	–	05/2008
Mixed governments				
Hamburg	CDU, Green	Yes	–	04/2010
Mecklenburg-West Pom.	CDU, SPD	Yes (planned)	–	~ 2011
Saarland	CDU, FDP, Green	Yes	–	09/2010
Saxony-Anhalt	CDU, SPD	No	–	–
Thuringia	SPD, CDU	Yes (planned)	–	09/2010 (draft)
Centre–left governments				
Berlin	SPD, Left	Yes	€7.50	06/2010
Brandenburg	SPD, Left	Yes (planned)	€7.50	08/2010 (draft)
Bremen	SPD, Green	Yes	€7.50	11/2009
North-Rhine Westphalia	SPD, Green	Yes (planned)	?	~ 2011
Rhineland-Palatinate	SPD	Yes	€8.50	11/2010

procurement which, eventually, was incorporated into Berlin's new public procurement law.

Once the first *Länder* had revised their public procurement legislation without new legal challenges arising, others started to emulate and fine-tune these reforms. Berlin's new legislation was cited regularly in parliamentary debates across different German *Länder* and was referred to explicitly in new legislative drafts.[6] In addition, reference to earlier reforms is made by non-governmental actors, mainly left opposition parties and trade unions, in order to demand similar reforms and to refute blame-shifting to the European level (Schulten 2010b: 12f.). Taken together, this has led to a trend from legally rather modest early reforms (e.g., Hamburg, Bremen) to bolder attempts of

Länder governments (e.g., Berlin, Rhineland-Palatinate) to explore the limits of their regulatory autonomy after *Rüffert.*

In particular, three elements recur in most post-*Rüffert* reforms (Schulten 2010a: 3). First, the requirement of collective agreement declarations was reintroduced, but limited to minimum wages in sectors covered by universally applicable collective agreements. Second, full compliance with the representative local collective agreement is still required in the transport sector which was legally not affected by the *Rüffert* judgment. Finally, specific minimum wages for public procurement have been introduced. Whereas their applicability has come to be generally regarded as in conformity with EU law, mainly on the basis of numerous legal surveys and the experience so far, this element has not yet had to survive a legal challenge in court (Rödl 2011).

In sum, *Rüffert* has provided centre–right *Länder* governments an opportunity to abolish or disapply the requirement of collective agreement declarations, but it has not ruled out entirely the possibility of including social provisions in public procurement legislation. Facing the threat of both further private litigation and infringement action of the Commission, *Länder* governments proceeded carefully: first, they suspended existing provisions and, then, they gradually explored new ways to legally include social considerations into public procurement legislation. Early *Länder* reforms were prepared by extensive legal surveys while later reforms could emulate the emerging post-*Rüffert* precedent. Today, more *Länder* have enacted legislation on collective agreement declarations, albeit less demanding than before the ECJ's ruling.

Commission vs Luxembourg: a strategy of 'trial and error'

At first sight, Luxembourg's legislative response to the ECJ's ruling in *Commission vs Luxembourg* comes close to 'regulatory surrender' as defined above. According to the explanatory memorandum to the revised law, the 'unique goal is to bring legislation in conformity with European jurisprudence'.[7] Article 1(1) of Luxembourg's original implementation of the PWD provided a list of 14 issues that were considered essential for the regulation of working conditions in general and also applied to posted workers. Four of these points were challenged by the European Commission as going beyond what was covered by the PWD and considered unjustified restrictions of European services freedom by the ECJ: the monitoring of written employment contracts; the automatic indexation of salaries; the rules on part-time and fixed-term work; and the regulation of collective labour agreements. In response to the ECJ's judgment, Luxembourg's legislative reform rendered these provisions inapplicable to posted workers and the Commission closed its infringement proceeding in October 2010.

The picture gets more nuanced, however, if we consider the motives for the original implementing law of 2002 and the revision process in 2010. Given that no legal precedent on the correct interpretation of the PWD existed in 2002, Luxembourg opted for a legislative strategy of 'trial and error', i.e., interpreting its autonomy to regulate posted work extensively first and, then, being taught about its limits by the ECJ. Moreover, a strategy of inclusion towards the Commission was deliberately rejected. François Biltgen, Luxembourg's minister of labour and employment responsible for drafting the original and the revised law, justifies the decision not to informally negotiate the original law with the Commission:[8]

> In fact, such negotiations would have just resulted in imposing a priori upon Luxembourg a 'neoliberal' interpretation of the Posted Workers Directive ... Instead, the government – with the consent of social partners and parliament – preferred to design the law according to its own vision of social Europe and national social public policy. [This approach] implied a certain risk of legal action by the Commission, although the Directorate General for Employment and Social Affairs, for its part, was not *a priori* opposed [...] The government was aware that a condemnation by the ECJ was possible.

Thus, the original law was written on the basis of a very broad interpretation of national regulatory autonomy, supported by societal consensus at home and speculating on internal dissent of the Commission. Instead of 'overimplementing' (Conant 2002: 70) the PWD in the absence of legal precedent, a calculated risk of legal challenge was deliberately taken.

The ECJ's judgment in *Commission vs Luxembourg* narrowed the interpretation of permissible public policy exceptions under the PWD and, in its response, Luxembourg's government refrained from further exploring uncertain legal territory.[9] Thus, the Court undoubtedly constrained domestic regulatory autonomy, but it did so in a rather limited way. Luxembourg's parliamentary committee of labour and employment concludes:[10]

> It needs to be emphasized that the judgment and the present reform are far from substantially endangering Luxembourg's social legislation. The reform introduces some necessary adjustments which preserve social legislation at the same time as clarifying its applicability to posted workers.

In sum, Luxembourg's legislative response to the ECJ's judgment was a step back from an initially very extensive interpretation of the PWD.

CONCLUSION

This contribution asked for member state governments' motives and strategies to regulate 'with Luxembourg in mind'. The ECJ's judgments in *Laval*, *Rüffert* and *Commission vs Luxembourg* seriously challenged domestic rules on posted workers. To avoid further conflicts and overcome legal uncertainty, member state governments could not ignore the rulings or 'contain' (Conant 2002) their impact to the individual cases, but had to engage in broader reforms. At the same time, the variety of national responses shows that they still had considerable room for manoeuvre and, thus, contradicts the gloomy forecasts of early legal commentaries on the judgments (Joerges and Rödl 2009; Kilpatrick

2009; Malmberg and Sigeman 2008). By including potential litigants in re-regulation and building on existing legal precedent, member state and *Länder* governments were able to preserve significant parts of their original legislation in EU-compatible ways. Their willingness and ability to apply these regulatory strategies varied, hence, Europe's 'differential' impact (Héritier 2001).

The analysis also showed that the ECJ and its rulings need to be put in context. Rather than intruding into stable political settlements, the Court was called to rule on long-standing controversies between and within member states. In *Laval* and *Rüffert*, domestic political battles were brought to the Court, and in *Commission vs Luxembourg* a government deliberately tested the European limits of national law. The final rulings may have ultimately settled some of the legal controversies, but they marked just one, albeit important, stage in the political contest. In response to the rulings, member state governments had to strike new balances between regulatory autonomy and EU-compatibility which have, so far, not been challenged again.

Focusing on domestic political responses to the European judiciary has been justified because of member states' difficulties in jointly reversing or complementing ECJ-driven integration. Unless balancing community and autonomy in the EU is to be left entirely to the dialogue of courts, member state governments often need to explore domestically their remaining autonomy. Ultimately, studying domestic responses to the ECJ also helps to better understand decisions taken at the EU level. First, the Court may become 'sensitized' to domestic concerns through member states' political responses and, accordingly, 'fine-tune' its own jurisprudence (Obermaier 2008: 26).[11] Second, national regulation adopted in direct response to the ECJ's jurisprudence may in the long run also shape political integration at the European level (Eichhorst 2000: 281). Domestic regulation 'with Luxembourg in mind' can serve as a model of autonomy-regarding integration at the EU level.

Biographical note: Michael Blauberger is assistant professor at the University of Salzburg, Salzburg Centre of European Union Studies (SCEUS).

ACKNOWLEDGEMENTS

I would like to thank two anonymous reviewers and Alexandre Afonso, Philipp Genschel, Marie-Pierre Granger, Miriam Hartlapp, Adrienne Héritier, Dan Kelemen, Juan Mayoral, Diana Panke, Susanne K. Schmidt, Anne Thies, Benjamin Werner and Rebecca Zahn for their comments. I am grateful to the Robert Schuman Centre for Advanced Studies for granting me a Jean Monnet Fellowship 2010/11 and to the German Research Foundation for its funding of the Collaborative Research Centre 597.

NOTES

1 In contrast to the other cases, *Viking* was decided on the basis of the freedom of establishment, which makes the case rather specific.

2 For a summary of their positions, see: 'Social partners have differing views on Laval Inquiry', available at http://www.eurofound.europa.eu/eiro/2009/05/articles/se0905029i.htm (accessed 10 May 2011).

3 Act on amendment of the Act on Posting of Workers, adopted 18 December 2008, entry into force 01 January 2009.

4 Changes to the Co-Determination Act and the Posting of Workers' Act, adopted 05 November 2009, entry into force 15 April 2010.

5 Anonymous interviews with representatives from the Swedish and Danish trade union confederations, 28 April and 4 May 2011.

6 Brandenburg's legislative draft (Landtag Brandenburg, Drucksache 5/3030) includes an extensive excursus on the EU-compatibility of the proposed legislation and several explicit references to Berlin. The parliamentary debate on minimum standards regarding public procurement in North-Rhine Westphalia (Landtag Nordrhein-Westfalen, Plenarprotokoll 15/16) witnessed multiple references to the reforms of other *Länder* governments and their legal expertise.

7 Loi du 11 avril 2010 portant modification des articles L. 010-1, L. 141-1, L. 142-2, L. 142-3 et L. 142-4 du Code du Travail. The law and the legislative process are documented in Dossier parlementaire No. 5942, available at http://www.chd.lu/wps/portal/public/RoleEtendu?action=doDocpaDetails&id=5942 (accessed 10 May 2011). For the citation, translated by the author, see page 12 in document 5942/00 'Exposé des motifs'.

8 See Endnote 7, page 5 in document 5942/00 'Exposé des motifs', translated by the author.

9 For example, the idea of limiting the definition of posted work temporally and with reference to tasks that are 'not part of the normal activity' of a company was dropped after a formal objection of the State Council which warned about new infringement action. See Endnote 10, pages 4–5 in document 5942/05 'Avis du Conseil d'Etat'.

10 See Endnote 7, page 7 in document 5942/00 'Rapport de la Commission du Travail et de l'Emploi', translated by the author.

11 Accordingly, in two more recent cases, the Court's Advocate Generals pleaded for an adjustment of the *Laval* and *Rüffert* jurisprudence, but the final judgements did not follow their opinions (Joerges 2011: 32–34).

REFERENCES

Börzel, T.A. (2003) 'Guarding the Treaty. The compliance strategies of the European Commission', in T.A. Börzel and R.A. Cichowski (eds), *Guarding the Treaty. The Compliance Strategies of the European Commission*, Oxford/New York: Oxford University Press, pp. 197–220.

Börzel, T.A. and Risse, T. (2007) 'Europeanization: the domestic impact of European Union politics', in K.E. Jørgensen, M.A. Pollack and B. Rosamond (eds), *Europeanization: The Domestic Impact of European Union Politics*, London: Sage Publications, pp. 483–504.

Bruun, N. and Jonsson, C.-M. (2010) 'Nordic countries', in A. Bücker and W. Warneck (eds), *Nordic Countries*, Brussels: European Trade Union Institute (ETUI), pp. 15–28.

Conant, L. (2002) *Justice Contained: Law and Politics in the European Union*, London/Ithaca, NY: Cornell University Press.

Danish Ministry of Employment (2008) *Betænkning fra udredningsarbejdet om Laval-afgørelsen*, Copenhagen.
Davesne, A. (2009) 'The Laval Case and the future of labour relations in Sweden', *Les Cahiers Européens No. 012009*, Paris: Sciences Po.
Eichhorst, W. (2000) *Europäische Sozialpolitik zwischen nationaler Autonomie und Marktfreiheit. Die Entsendung von Arbeitnehmern in der EU*, Frankfurt a.M: Campus.
Eurofound (2010) *Posted Workers in the European Union*, Dublin: European Foundation for the Improvement of Living and Working Conditions.
European Social Partners (2010) *Report on Joint Work of the European Social Partners on the ECJ rulings in the Viking, Laval, Rüffert and Luxembourg Cases*, Brussels.
Genschel, P. and Jachtenfuchs, M. (2011) 'How the European Union constrains the state: multilevel governance of taxation', *European Journal of Political Research* 50(1): 293–314.
Hänlein, A., Jordan, R. and Sack, D. (2008) *Abschlussbericht: Tariftreuegesetze vor der Novellierung oder Abschaffung? Die Folgen der Rechtsprechung des Europäischen Gerichtshofes (C-346/06)*, Bielefeld: Fakultät für Soziologie.
Hartlapp, M. and Falkner, G. (2009) 'Problems of operationalization and data in EU compliance research', *European Union Politics* 10(2): 281–304.
Héritier, A. (2001) 'Differential Europe: the European Union impact on national policymaking', in A. Héritier *et al.* (eds), *Differential Europe: The European Union Impact on National Policymaking*, Lanham, MD: Rowman & Littlefield, pp. 1–21.
Joerges, C. (2011) 'Unity in diversity as Europe's vocation and conflicts law as Europe's constitutional form', *TranState Working Papers No. 148*, Bremen.
Joerges, C. and Rödl, F. (2009) 'Informal politics, formalised law and the "Social Deficit" of European integration: reflections after the judgments of the ECJ in Viking and Laval', *European Law Journal* 15(1): 1–19.
Kelemen, R.D. (2011) *Eurolegalism. The Transformation of Law and Regulation in the European Union*, Cambridge, MA: Harvard University Press.
Kilpatrick, C. (2009) 'Laval's regulatory conundrum: collective standard-setting and the Court's new approach to posted workers', *European Law Journal* 34(6): 844–65.
Lindstrom, N. (2010) 'Service liberalization in the enlarged EU: a race to the bottom or the emergence of transnational political conflict?', *Journal of Common Market Studies* 48(5): 1307–27.
Malmberg, J. (2010) 'Posting post Laval. International and national responses', *Working Paper 2010: 5*, Uppsala: Uppsala Center for Labor Studies.
Malmberg, J. and Sigeman, T. (2008) 'Industrial actions and EU economic freedoms: the autonomous collective bargaining model curtailed by the European Court of Justice', *Common Market Law Review* 45(4): 1115–46.
Martinsen, D.S. and Vrangbæk, K. (2008) 'The Europeanization of health care governance: implementing the market imperatives of Europe', *Public Administration* 86(1): 169–84.
Mayer, F.C. (2009) 'Der EuGH und das soziale Europa', in Friedrich Ebert Stiftung (ed.), *Der EuGH und das soziale Europa*, Berlin: Friedrich Ebert Stiftung, pp. 7–25.
Neergaard, U. and Nielsen, R. (2010) 'Blurring boundaries: from the Danish welfare state to the European Social Model?', *European Labour Law Journal* 1(4): 434–88.
Obermaier, A.J. (2008) 'Fine-tuning the jurisprudence: the ECJ's judicial activism and self-restraint', *Working Paper No. 02/2008*, Vienna.
Rödl, F. (2009) 'The ECJ's Rüffert-judgement: a case for "undistorted" wage competition', *Harvard European Law Working Paper No. 01/2009*, Cambridge, MA.
Rödl, F. (2011) 'Bezifferte Mindestentgeltvorgaben im Vergaberecht', *Europäische Zeitschrift für Wirtschaftsrecht* 22(8): 292–96.
Rönnmar, M. (2010) 'Laval returns to Sweden: the final judgment of the Swedish Labour Court and Swedish legislative reforms', *Industrial Law Journal* 39(3): 280–87.

Sack, D. (2010) 'Europäisierungsdruck und Parteiendifferenz in den deutschen Bundesländern. Die Rechtsprechung des EuGH und die Novellierung von Tariftreueregelungen', *Politische Vierteljahresschrift* 51(4): 619–42.
Scharpf, F.W. (2009a) 'The double asymmetry of European integration, or: why the EU cannot be a social market economy', *MPIfG Working Paper 09/12*, Cologne.
Scharpf, F.W. (2009b) 'Legitimacy in the multilevel European polity', *European Political Science Review* 1(2): 173–204.
Schmidt, S.K. (2000) 'Only an agenda setter? The European Commission's power over the Council of Ministers', *European Union Politics* 1(1): 37–61.
Schmidt, S.K., Blauberger, M. and van den Nouland, W. (2008) 'Jenseits von Implementierung und Compliance. Die Europäisierung der Mitgliedstaaten', in I. Tömmel (ed.), *Jenseits von Implementierung und Compliance. Die Europäisierung der Mitgliedstaaten*, Wiesbaden: VS Verlag für Sozialwissenschaften, pp. 275–96.
Schulten, T. (2010a) 'Comeback der Tariftreue', *Böckler impuls* 2010(12): 3.
Schulten, T. (2010b) *Stellungnahme zum Antrag der Fraktion DIE LINKE: 'Mindestanforderungen an ein Tariftreue- und Vergabegesetz Nordrhein-Westfalen'*, Düsseldorf: Hans-Böckler Stiftung.
Slagter, T.H. (2009) 'National parliaments and the ECJ: a view from the Bundestag', *Journal of Common Market Studies* 47(1): 175–97.
Stone Sweet, A. (2010) 'The European Court of Justice and the judicialization of EU governance', *Living Reviews in European Governance* 5(2), available at http://europeangovernance.livingreviews.org/Articles/lreg-2010-2/
Stone Sweet, A. and Brunell, T.L. (2010) 'Overriding the European Court of Justice? Qualitative evidence from cases in the Carruba, Gabel, and Hankla data set (1987–1997)', *Public Law Working Paper No. 217*, New Haven, CT: Yale Law School.
Swedish Government (2008) *Action in Response to the Laval Judgment. Summary*, Stockholm: Swedish Government Official Reports.
Tallberg, J. (2002) 'Delegation to supranational institutions: why, how, and with what consequences?', *West European Politics* 25(1): 23–46.
Töller, A.E. (2004) 'The Europeanization of public policies: understanding idiosyncratic mechanisms and contingent results', *European Integration Online Papers* 8(9), available at http://eiop.or.at/eiop/pdf/2004-009.pdf
Töller, A.E. (2010) 'Measuring and comparing the Europeanization of national legislation: a research note', *Journal of Common Market Studies* 48(2): 417–44.
Treib, O. (2003) 'Die Umsetzung von EU-Richtlinien im Zeichen der Parteipolitik: Eine akteurzentrierte Antwort auf die Misfit-These', *Politische Vierteljahresschrift* 44(4): 506–28.
Wind, M. (2010) 'The Nordics, the EU and the reluctance towards supranational judicial review', *Journal of Common Market Studies* 48(4): 1039–63.
Woolfson, C., Thörnqvist, C. and Sommers, J. (2010) 'The Swedish model and the future of labour standards after Laval', *Industrial Relations Journal* 41(4): 333–50.

Perpetual momentum: directed and unconstrained?

Fritz W. Scharpf

ABSTRACT At the most general level, the perpetual momentum of 'integration through law' is driven by the substantive dynamics of legal doctrines extending the protection of individual interests and by procedural conditions facilitating the use of European law to challenge the institutional regimes of EU member states. Given the supremacy and direct effect of European law, and the decision rules of EU policy making, this momentum could not be halted through political or judicial intervention.

INTRODUCTION: THE CONTINGENCY OF THE COURT'S POWER

The European Court of Justice (ECJ) as the 'Motor of Integration' promoting a 'Europe of Rights' – these have become generally accepted descriptors in affirmative or critical accounts of the role of 'Integration through Law' in the constitutional development of the European Union (EU). Contributions in the present collection do challenge the descriptive generality of the underlying assumptions; they help to identify the areas where they do in fact apply; and they reconstruct the mechanisms and the conditions on which their empirical effectiveness depends. In my reflections on this collection I will not review the individual contributions. Instead, I will suggest some observations on the domain, the direction and the impact of the Court's 'constitutional-court function' in the multi-level European polity.

At the outset it needs to be acknowledged that the dominant focus on the ECJ's active role in widening the domain of legal integration tends to underestimate the importance of its more ordinary 'high-court functions' as well as the precariousness of the Court's powers. The European Union, lacking an administrative infrastructure of its own, has come to rely on private litigants and national courts to ensure the effectiveness of its (constitutionally undisputed) legislative powers (Kelemen 2011). As a consequence, as Damian Chalmers and Mariana Chaves (2012) show, monitoring and guiding the interpretation and application of European legislation through national courts does indeed constitute a major part of the ECJ's ordinary business. At the same time, however, Gareth Davies (2012) emphasizes the precarious nature of these supervisory powers. Unlike national high courts, the ECJ is not positioned at the apex of an integrated judicial hierarchy. Even though European law is to be treated as supreme 'law of the land' in all EU member states, litigants cannot appeal from national courts, and the ECJ cannot reverse their judgments. To come into play at all, it depends on preliminary-reference requests; and the effect of its rulings depends on the use that national courts will make of them. In short, therefore, the effectiveness of the Court's role in the enforcement of European law is contingent on the support of national judiciaries, and it may vary across national judicial cultures.

THE LIMITS OF POLITICAL INTERFERENCE

In comparison to national high courts, however, there seem to be very few constraints on the ECJ's capacity to interpret and shape the substance of European law in the cases that come before it. Daniel Kelemen (2012) persuasively argues that none of the political constraints on judicial independence that have been discussed in the American literature could be employed to influence the ECJ. Given the extremely high consensus requirements of EU legislation and Treaty amendments, the possibility of legislative, let alone constitutional, override is as remote as are threats of jurisdiction stripping, resource punishment or court packing that would all require the unanimous agreement of 27 member states. In an ingenious thought experiment Kelemen also shows that, even if they tried, national governments would hardly be able to influence ECJ decisions through the strategic use of individual judicial appointments. Moreover, drawing on Eurobarometer data which suggest that popular 'trust' is comparatively high for the ECJ and much lower for national governments, parliaments and political parties,[1] Kelemen also suggests that public opinion would not support governments confronting or openly disobeying ECJ decisions. Given the normative commitment to a 'rule of law' and the mystique of courts 'saying what the law is', I would agree.

However, the fact that the ECJ is institutionally well protected against political interference merely implies a comparatively high potential for judicial law-making. That it is in fact used, and employed with strong pro-integration effect, is shown by Michael Malecki (2012). Based on a dataset including all 1,549 preliminary-reference decisions between 1970 and 1997 in which the Commission did announce a position, he finds that the Court sided with the Commission in about 75 per cent of the cases – which he interprets as a strong pro-integration tendency. And while significant differences among individual judges are revealed through sophisticated statistical analysis, even the least pro-European judge has supported the Commission in 72 per cent of the cases in which he or she participated. That seems strong evidence in search of strong explanations. In this context, reference is often made to hypotheses about the – neo-liberal and/or pro-European – preferences and interests of individual judges (e.g., Chalmers 1997; Höpner 2010) or to their inclusion in the Euro-law epistemic community (Alter 2009; Vauchez 2007). The present collection bypasses such attempts to assess individual subjectivities in favour of structural, institutional and contextual explanations.

A MODEL OF JUDICIAL ACTIVISM

Susanne Schmidt's (2012) contribution, in particular, represents an ambitious attempt to explain both, the ECJ's judicial activism and its pro-integration tendency, in a two-stage model of dynamic and directed path dependence. The first stage of this model amounts to a reconstruction of the logic of legal reasoning in a case-law system. There, the principles of *stare decisis* and of precedent serve to ensure the inter-temporal stability of judge-made law by requiring that, in the absence of massive countervailing considerations, the legal rule announced in one case also ought to be applied in factually similar later cases. At the same time, however, judges are also expected to guard the consistency of the case-law system across lines of cases. This implies that innovative decisions ought to be guided by a Kantian 'categorical imperative' favouring rules that could be generalized. And in order to minimize *ad hoc* decisions, cases that are not directly covered by precedent should still be decided by reference to previously established rules which may serve as a 'heuristic principle' in the search for appropriate solutions – and will thus contribute to the ideal of an internally consistent legal order that is being discovered, rather than made, by judges (Esser 1964: ch. X). In a case-law system, therefore, the set of rules announced in previous decisions will be associated with a penumbra of potential extrapolations which might be invoked in different, but arguably analogous, case constellations in other fields.

The second stage of Schmidt's (2012) model focuses on individuals, firms and other organizations for which not only the settled case law, but also its penumbra of potential extensions, represents an opportunity structure. If they find it worthwhile to advance their interests by invoking European law in ordinary litigation, and if the interpretation of the European rule is not yet definitely settled by precedents, the national court may refer the question[2] to the ECJ for a preliminary ruling. By implication, therefore, the flow of legal issues that are presented to the Court through the preliminary-reference procedure must be shaped by a double selectivity: the requests will be driven by litigants seeking an advancement of their individual interests beyond the limits established by existing national law – rather than by litigants whose interests are protected by national law; and the Court will only see requests that seek an extension of European law beyond the limits defined by previous ECJ precedents. That does of course not imply that all of these requests will be granted. But given the supremacy of European law over all national law, and given the supremacy of Treaty law over European legislation, any decision in which such a request is in fact successful will extend the reach of European law with a 'ratcheting effect' that is protected against political reversal, and that could be judicially reversed only if the Court would explicitly overrule its own precedent. In the abstract, therefore, Susanne Schmidt's two-stage model does predict a tendency of the ECJ case law to dynamically extend the protection of individual interests through European law – and thus to promote 'Integration through Law' as well as a 'Europe of Rights'.

More specifically, Schmidt (2012) uses this model to explain a path-dependent evolution of ECJ case law originating from the highly innovative *Cassis* decision. There, the Court had applied the Treaty commitments to the free movement of goods not only to measures discriminating against imports but to all national rules which, if they differed from one country to another, were seen as 'non-tariff barriers' that might impede the exercise of free-movement rights. If such rules could not be justified by reference to a limited number of Court-defined 'mandatory requirements' combined with a strict proportionality test, the new rule would be 'mutual recognition' – whereby free access had to be granted to all products lawfully introduced in their country of origin. Schmidt further describes how the combined principles of non-discrimination (on grounds of nationality) and of non-restriction (of free movement) have subsequently been extended to the other economic liberties (services, capital, workers and establishment) in spite of significant differences in the underlying *problematique*.

Thus, the Court, emphasizing 'non-restriction', applied the *country-of-origin rule* not only to regulations of product quality, but also to services and capital – where the expectation that host countries could rely on the home-country regulation and supervision of mobile capital and financial services was never plausible. By contrast, 'non-discrimination' is emphasized to ensure the strict application of *host-country rules* where the free movement of workers and the freedom of establishment are at stake. And as the Court continued to extend free movement rights from workers to their family members, to job-seekers, to students and, finally, to all citizens of EU member states, it also went beyond the logic of market integration. In effect, the Court is promoting social integration by rapidly increasing the access of economically inactive migrants to the full range of benefits that national welfare states have come to provide and finance for their own citizens.

LITIGANTS, ECONOMIC RIGHTS, AND THE LIMITS OF SOLIDARITY

These extensions of free-mobility rights are well explained by Schmidt's two-stage model – but obviously their dynamic evolution and its directions are driven by very different groups of litigants (including, of course, the Commission when it is intervening against member state regulations through infringement prosecutions). The contribution of Damian Chalmers and Mariana Chaves (2012) provides an extremely interesting and useful cross-tabulation representing the involvement of five classes of litigants involved in preliminary-reference decisions dealing with 20 different sub-fields of European law.

At the same time, however, the dynamic extension of the non-restriction and non-discrimination principles through the free-movement decisions of the ECJ raises fundamental issues concerning the EU's constitutional architecture that are difficult to resolve within the Court's established framework of legal reasoning. The first of these issues is highlighted by the fact that, in Chalmers and Chaves's (2012) cross-tabulation, 'domestic firms' constitute a large segment of the litigants in the free-movement fields (and in taxation) – which the authors find puzzling since 'competition, free movement of services and freedom of establishment all require, in principle, the presence or imminence of transnational trade for their instigation'. Under the Court's definition of free-movement rights, however, such constraints do not play a role.

Since, according to the formula announced in *Dassonville* and re-affirmed in *Cassis*, the exercise of free-movement rights is protected against all national measures '*which are capable of hindering directly or indirectly, actually of potentially, intra-Community trade*' (8/74 at #5; emphasis added) (and since the ECJ has no restrictive rules on 'standing to raise the issue'), the identification of 'indirect' or 'potential' restrictions does indeed not depend on litigants that are themselves involved in any border-crossing transactions. But if neither protectionist discrimination nor a manifest impact on transnational economic interactions is required, the prohibition of all measures that may be '*liable to hinder or make less attractive the exercise of the fundamental freedoms*' (*Gebhard* C-55/94; emphasis added) will logically turn into judicial control of all national rules and practices that regulate or burden domestic economic activities as such (because these, by logical implication, might also reduce the attractiveness of inward mobility).

As a consequence, free-movement rights provide the Court with general powers to require the deregulation and liberalization of national economic regimes – and thereby to displace the political choices of EU member states through a judicially defined 'economic constitution'.[3] With regard to the free movement of goods, where national standards on product quality have largely been replaced by European legislation on consumer and environmental protection, that may appear as a minor problem. But that is not true of the case law regarding free capital movement and establishment, where highly salient differences among national 'varieties of capitalism' have impeded political re-regulation at the European level. It is the case law, therefore, rather than legislation, that has greatly reduced the capacity of member states to shape and defend specific national regimes of corporate governance (Höpner and Schäfer 2010), to tax the profits of domestically producing corporations or to promote economic development through 'services of general economic interest'. In other words, European 'social market economies' are being transformed into liberal market economies (Scharpf 2010) primarily by the Court's extension of the 'non-restriction' principle.

By contrast, market-liberalizing effects are less important or even lacking in the case law extending the free-movement rights of workers, job-seekers, students, patients and, finally, citizens. To be sure, the free movement of workers was intended to complement economic integration by creating a European labour market[4] and the case law extending patient rights (Sindbjerg Martinsen and Vrangbaek 2008) might also contribute to creating a European market for health care services. But such effects would matter less and less as mobility rights are conferred on students[5] and other economically inactive migrants and, finally, on citizens in general (Wollenschläger 2011). In any case, however, the effect of these decisions is not negative integration and deregulation in the name of market freedoms. Instead, they are meant to establish positive claims of migrants (or migrant consumers) to the social benefits and services of existing national welfare states,

In that sense, decisions extending the equal-treatment rights of mobile persons may indeed be interpreted as extending the reach of market-correcting solidarity (Caporaso and Tarrow 2009). At the same time, however, the logic of non-discrimination on grounds of nationality does not reflect the 'club-goods' character of collectively financed welfare regimes which member states have created for their own citizens and permanent residents. By extending their coverage to non-members, the case law may engender fears of 'welfare migration' in states with high levels of redistribution – which may then provoke either xenophobic political reactions or undermine the commitment to, and the generosity of, solidaristic welfare systems (Menéndez 2009; Somek 2008a). Beyond that, however, the Court's reference to both of the *Cassis* principles (non-restriction as well as non-discrimination) in its citizenship decisions implies the possibility that these may also be applied – just as is true in the case law on economic liberties – in cases that do not involve transnational mobility at all. If that should come to pass, any national regulation that restricts individual freedom domestically may also be challenged as a restriction to the exercise of European citizenship rights – which would radically liberalize not only the economic regimes but also the social orders of all EU member states (Wollenschläger 2011).[6] That is not meant to suggest that the Court will soon go to extremes in challenging the normative foundations of national societies. Yet, what stands in the way of litigant pressures are at best the discretionary obstacles of the proportionality test.

LITIGANTS AND ANTI-DISCRIMINIATION

The contribution of Alec Stone Sweet and Kathleen Stranz (2012) introduces a third category of expansionary case law that differs from both the economic and the non-economic free-movement cases discussed by Susanne Schmidt (2012). These decisions are definitely not about negative integration – in fact, they are not about European integration at all. They also serve no deregulatory or liberalizing purpose. Instead, the German statute that was seen to violate the ECJ's newly-found 'fundamental right' against age discrimination in the *Mangold* case had in fact liberalized existing employment protection legislation in order to improve the employability of older workers. At the same time, these cases are not, or at least not primarily, about widening the access to welfare state benefits. Instead, non-discrimination is invoked to achieve inter-personal equality *per se*, regardless of whether unequal treatment is imposed by the state or by non-state actors.

It is clear that these cases cannot be explained as a path-dependent unfolding of the principles adopted in *Cassis*. While they should also be seen as the product of a litigation-driven evolution from principles announced in early precedents, their starting position was not defined by the free-movement clauses of the European Economic Community Treaty, but by the requirement of equal pay for men and women (Art. 119 EEC). Again, however, the case law quickly extended the principle to non-pay-related aspects of employment and to non-employment-related aspects of gender equality. In the process, moreover, the definition was enlarged to include 'indirect discrimination' and the principle was also applied with 'horizontal direct effect' to contractual relations between employers and employees (Cichowski 2007). In this regard, a high point was reached in the recent '*Unisex*' decision (C-236/09) where the ECJ invalidated a Council Directive that had allowed insurance contracts to reflect statistical differences in the life expectancy (or the accident proneness) of men and women.

As Stone Sweet and Stranz (2012) are pointing out, whenever the Court is applying Treaty-based rights with horizontal direct effect, it is in fact engaging in 'positive integration' by imposing a common European rule on private contractual relationships. In the *Unisex* case, it is in fact installing common European rules requiring solidaristic redistribution – where men must subsidize the life insurance of women while cautious women drivers will subsidize the accident insurance of reckless males. In functional terms, this appears as an extreme case of judicial legislation, far removed from a textual base in the Treaty and overriding even the explicit political choice of a Council Directive. Normatively, however, these cases on interpersonal non-discrimination cannot be supported by the usual legitimating discourses hailing the Court as a 'Motor of Integration'. At best, they may represent a contribution to the ideal of a 'Europe of rights' (Kelemen 2011).

It is this ideal which could in fact be employed on the one hand as a normative justification and on the other hand as a functional explanation in a model that tries to account for active judicial law-making on economic as well as non-economic mobility rights, and also on fundamental rights that involve neither economic liberties nor transnational mobility. What these seemingly disparate fields of ECJ case law have in common is the fact that the Court's law-making power does depend on the creation of individual rights. The foundation of this power was laid already in 1963, in the *Van Gend en Loos* (26/62) decision where the Court introduced the doctrine of 'direct effect' by interpreting a Treaty rule on tariffs as '*creating individual rights which national courts must protect*' (emphasis added). In the constitutional structure of multilevel Europe, this was the crucial linchpin. In the absence of Treaty-based individual rights with direct effectiveness and supremacy, the preliminary-reference procedure could never have achieved its litigation-driven dynamism. The 'Motor of Integration' could only have worked through Treaty amendments and Council directives; and member state governments would have remained 'Masters of the Treaty', rather than finding themselves pushed forward and at the same time constrained by the judicial power to promote 'Integration through Law' and a 'Europe of Rights'.

CONCLUSION: THE ECJ AND THE SKEWED CONSTITUTIONAL BALANCE

While the Court's contribution to European integration is widely considered beneficial in politically correct discourses, its impact on the constitutional balance of the multilevel European polity does raise serious problems. At the most fundamental level, all constitutional democracies must try to balance 'republican' principles emphasizing political self-determination and 'liberal' principles providing constitutional and judicial protection for certain individual rights. If this balance is upset by the 'perpetual momentum' of ECJ case law that is consistently extending the domain of constitutionally protected individual rights – and hence the range of issues that are placed beyond the reach of democratic self-determination – the legitimacy of the multilevel European polity itself may be undermined (Scharpf 2009). The question is whether there are, or could be, countervailing mechanisms that would defend or restore the constitutional balance.

Political remedies are unlikely to succeed. For reasons demonstrated in Kelemen's (2012) contribution, member states will be unable to oppose the Court directly, and even though governments may be able to gain some relief through the practices of 'creative' evasion and passive resistance described by Michael Blauberger (2012), these will remain vulnerable to litigation by 'private prosecutors' and the judgments of national courts which governments could not ignore without disavowing their allegiance to the rule of law (Kelemen 2011). Possibly, however, the very fact that national courts must play a crucial role in the European legal system might also allow them to shield national polities and their constitutional balance against the unbalancing impact of ECJ decisions.

That the potential for such a protective role does exist is shown in Gareth Davies's (2012) contribution. In preliminary-reference decisions, the Court is responding to questions of law, rather than deciding cases. And its responses typically include 'open norms' (including the criteria of the proportionality test) whose application to the facts of the case leaves a good deal of room for the judgment of the referring court. Moreover, it is the national court that must decide whether to ask for a preliminary reference in the first place, and it will also phrase the questions to which the ECJ may respond. In fact, comparative research has found significant differences in the frequency of preliminary references originating from courts in different member states, and it has shown that, in particular, courts in Scandinavian countries seem to be more reluctant to challenge the legislation of democratically legitimated national parliaments than is true of judges in post-fascist states on the European continent (Wind *et al.* 2009). However, Michael Blauberger (2012) reports that the

Danish legislature responded to the *Laval* decision even though Denmark was not a party to this case and, more generally, that law-abiding governments tend to take account of rules announced in ECJ precedents regardless of their immediate involvement.[7]

In any case, however, the reluctance of Scandinavian judges to challenge their own parliaments is not generally shared by national courts – which often seem eager to participate in the powers of judicial review which otherwise would be reserved to national constitutional or high courts (Alter 2001; Stone Sweet 2004). This is dramatically illustrated by Stone Sweet and Stranz (2012) in their fascinating account of how the ECJ's *Mangold* decision (C-144/04) represents a famous victory of German labour courts defending their aggressive case law on non-discrimination not only against liberalizing legislation but also against the constitutional court's more restrained reading of 'general equality'. There is, however, a further and more fundamental implication of this particular story.

In its decision on the *Lisbon* Treaty, the *Bundesverfassungsgericht*[8] had set itself up as the ultimate protector of national 'constitutional identity', including its foundation in the principle of democratic self-determination. Moreover, it had asserted its competence, and announced its intention, to protect these principles not only against European legislation exceeding the powers conferred by the member states, but also against creeping' extensions through overly extensive interpretations of delegated powers (at # 242). Since in Germany the ECJ's *Mangold* decision had been prominently denounced as a clear case of *ultra-vires* interpretation (Herzog and Gerken 2008),[9] whereas the constitutional court's *Lisbon* judgment was no less violently criticized as a reversion to constitutional nationalism, the first occasion where the *Bundesverfassungsgericht* would have to deal with the *Mangold* rule raised expectations of high drama (Gerken *et al.* 2009).

As one ought to have expected, however, when the occasion arose just a year later in the *Honeywell* decision,[10] the constitutional court found nothing wrong with *Mangold*: realizing that the uniform application of European law would be impossible if all national courts would generally apply their own constitutional standards (at # 57), the court refrained from attempting its own interpretation of European rights. Even if the ECJ's decision might not have been reached through accepted methods of legal interpretation (at # 68), it would have to be accepted unless it would change the structure of competences in major ways or impose significant burdens on (national) basic rights (at # 66). This the ECJ's *Mangold* decision had not done in 'obvious and structure-changing' ways. Under this standard, the dissenting opinion pointed out, the *Bundesverfassungsgericht* will never be able to intervene against the 'creeping' erosion of national autonomy through judicial interpretation. And given the direct effect and supremacy of ECJ case law, its impact will not be constrained by explicit allocations of competences[11] or by subsidiarity clauses in the Treaties.[12]

The ultimate reason for this defeat is constituted by the shared commitment of both courts to the protection of individual rights. As the ECJ's dynamic extension of European law proceeds not through decisions widening European legislative competences but through the expansion of *individual rights*, the *Bundesverfassungsgericht* could only oppose it on individual-rights grounds as well. Thus, when it had first challenged the supremacy of European law in order to protect the 'identity' of the German constitution in its 1974 *Solange I*[13] decision, it had focused on the Basic Law's catalogue of basic rights which it would have to guard 'as long as' European law did not provide similar guaranties. By 1986, however, in *Solange II*,[14] the German court had to acknowledge that the ECJ had in the meantime[15] developed its own fundamental rights jurisprudence by reference to the common constitutional tradition of EU member states – and so it announced that it would now refrain from exercising its own basic-rights review 'as long as' effective European review was ensured.

In other words, the court has accepted, and actually invited, the ECJ's power to define European individual rights – and in its own role as the champion of basic rights, it may at best compete with the ECJ for more protection, but it cannot intervene to defeat individual rights in the interest of political power (or democratic self-determination). In fact, the only potentially relevant objection to *Mangold* the court raised (and quickly dismissed) in *Honeywell* was that the European rule against age discrimination might violate employers' freedom of contract under the German constitution. Hence, competition between European and national individual rights might still play a role in the dialogue between the ECJ and national constitutional courts. But national courts cannot be expected to constrain the impact of a case law that dynamically extends the domain of protected individualism at the expense of political capacities for collective self-determination (Somek 2008b).[16] In effect, therefore, the 'perpetual momentum' is likely to go on.

Biographical note: Fritz W. Scharpf is Director Emeritus at the Max Planck Institute for the Study of Societies, Cologne.

NOTES

1 The comparative interpretation of these differences is not obvious, however. In a democracy, political parties, parliaments and governments are supposed to be involved in competition, public contestation and controversy – which implies that their legitimacy cannot be primarily based on 'trust'. By contrast, the legitimacy of institutions that are not democratically accountable depends entirely on trust in their integrity and competence – and it would quickly erode if they became embattled in serious controversies.

2 Since the ECJ is only responding to questions of law defined by the national court, it will not consider procedural criteria of 'standing', 'ripeness' and other requirements of a genuine 'case and controversy' – which the US Supreme Court employs to

avoid decisions on insufficiently clarified constitutional issues (Bickel 1962; Scharpf 1966).

3 The parallel to the pre-1937 US Supreme Court's use of the 'economic due process' doctrine to prevent all economic regulation (cf. Ehmke 1961; McCloskey 1962; Scharpf 1966) has been noted and criticized by Miguel P. Maduro (1998).

4 The free movement of workers is meant to ensure equality between migrant and domestic workers, whereas the free movement of services protects the right of employers to use 'posted workers' under conditions that are inferior to those enjoyed by domestic workers.

5 Interestingly, when patients are seeking healthcare abroad (invoking the freedom of receiving services), it is their home state that is held responsible for the reimbursement of costs, whereas the host state has to bear the cost when students are seeking education abroad (invoking the prohibition of discrimination on grounds of nationality).

6 It should be noted that in the transition from an authoritarian past in Germany, the constitutional court's interpretation of basic rights has played a very significant liberalizing role. The question is, however, whether the judicial transformation of national societies can be legitimately performed by the European rather than the national high court.

7 If an ECJ precedent seems to undermine the legality of a particular national law, the government's law-abidingness is likely to be challenged by the opposition (and possibly by a coalition party) – with effects on public opinion that are pointed out in Kelemen's (2012) contribution.

8 BVerfG, 2 BvR 2/08, 30.06.2009.

9 The senior author, Roman Herzog, was not only a former president of the *Bundesverfassungsgericht* but had also been president of the Convention that had drafted the EU's Charter of Fundamental Rights.

10 BVerfG, 2BvR 2661/06, 06.07.2010.

11 The ECJ's standard response is that, yes, the regulation of healthcare, etc., is left to member states, but in exercising their powers these must of course respect the Treaty-based rights of individuals. See, for example, *Kohll* (C-158/96 at # 16, 19-20).

12 However, the ECJ's individual-rights adjudication has the power to shape the course of European legislation (Scharpf 2011; Schmidt 2011).

13 BVerfGE 37, 271.

14 BVerfGE 73, 339.

15 The development occurred arguably in response to this and similar assertions of national constitutional courts (Weiler and Lockhart 1995).

16 In German constitutional adjudication, the court is of course aware of, and pays attention to, the requirements of democratic governance when it defines the limits of individual-rights protection in the specific case. But since it never saw a need to explicate these implicit limits in terms of a 'political question doctrine' (Scharpf 1966), they are of no use in conflicts with the ECJ. In legal as in other battles, one cannot beat something with nothing.

REFERENCES

Alter, K.J. (2001) *Establishing the Supremacy of European Law*, Oxford: Oxford University Press.

Alter, K.J. (2009) 'Jurist advocacy movements in Europe: the role of euro-law associations in European integration (1953–1975)', in K.J. Alter (ed.), *The European Court's Political Power*, Oxford: Oxford University Press, pp. 63–91.

Bickel, A.M. (1962) *The Least Dangerous Branch. The Supreme Court at the Bar of Politics*, Indianapolis, IN: Bobbs-Merrill.
Blauberger, M. (2012) 'With Luxembourg in mind . . . the remaking of national policies in the face of ECJ jurisprudence', *Journal of European Public Policy* 19(1): 109–26.
Caporaso, J.A. and Tarrow, S. (2009) 'Polanyi in Brussels: supranational institutions and the transnational embedding of markets', *International Organization* 63(4): 593–620.
Chalmers, D. (1997) 'Judicial preferences and the Community legal order', *The Modern Law Review* 60(2): 164–99.
Chalmers, D. and Chaves, M. (2012) 'The reference points of EU judicial politics', *Journal of European Public Policy* 19(1): 25–42.
Cichowski, R. (2007) *The European Court and Civil Society: Litigation, Mobilization and Governance*, Cambridge: Cambridge University Press.
Davies, G. (2012) 'Activism relocated: the self-restraint of the European Court of Justice in its national context', *Journal of European Public Policy* 19(1): 76–91.
Ehmke, H. (1961) *Wirtschaft und Verfassung. Die Verfassungsrechtsprechung des Supreme Court zur Wirtschaftsregulierung*, Karlsruhe: C.F. Müller.
Esser, J. (1964) *Grundsatz und Norm in der richterlichen Fortbildung des Privatrechts*, Tübingen: J.C.B. Mohr.
Gerken, L., Rieble, V., Roth, G.H., Stein, T. and Streinz, R. (2009) *„Mangold" als ausbrechender Rechtsakt*, Munich: Sellier.
Herzog, R. and Gerken, L. (2008) 'Stoppt den Europäischen Gerichtshof', *Frankfurter Allgemeine Zeitung*, 8 September.
Höpner, M. (2010) 'Warum betreibt der Europäische Gerichtshof Rechtsfortbildung? Die Politisierungshypothese', *Working Paper 10/2*, Cologne: Max Planck Institute for the Study of Societies, available at http://www.mpifg.de/pu/workpap/wp10-2.pdf (accessed 7 September 2011).
Höpner, M. and Schäfer, A. (2010) 'A new phase of European integration: organized capitalisms in post-Ricardian Europe', *West European Politics* 33(2): 344–68.
Kelemen, R.D. (2011) *Eurolegalism. The Transformation of Law and Regulation in the European Union*, Cambridge, MA: Harvard University Press.
Kelemen, R.D. (2012) 'The political foundations of judicial independence in the European Union', *Journal of European Public Policy* 19(1): 43–58.
Maduro, M.P. (1998) *We the Court: The European Court of Justice and the European Economic Constitution*, Oxford: Hart Publishers.
Malecki, M. (2012) 'Do ECJ judges all speak with the same voice? Evidence of divergent preferences from the judgments of chambers', *Journal of European Public Policy* 19(1): 59–75.
McCloskey, R.G. (1962) 'Economic due process and the Supreme Court: an exhumation and a reburial', *The Supreme Court Review* 1962: 34–62.
Menéndez, A.J. (2009) 'European citizenship after Martinez Sala and Baumbast: has European law become more human and less social?', *RECON Online Working Paper 2009/05*.
Scharpf, F.W. (1966) 'Judicial review and the political question – a functional analysis', *Yale Law Journal* 75(4): 517–98.
Scharpf, F.W. (2009) 'Legitimacy in the multilevel European polity', *European Political Science Review* 1(2): 173–204.
Scharpf, F.W. (2010) 'The asymmetry of European integration, or why the EU cannot be a "Social Market Economy"', *Socio-Economic Review* 8(2): 211–50.
Scharpf, F.W. (2011) 'The JDT model: context and extensions', in G. Falkner (ed.), *The EU's Decision Traps. Comparing Policies*, Oxford: Oxford University Press, pp. 217–36.

Schmidt, S.K. (2011) 'Overcoming the joint-decision trap in single-market legislation: the interplay between judicial and legislative politics', in G. Falkner (ed.), *The EU's Decision Traps. Comparing Policies*, Oxford: Oxford University Press, pp. 38–53.
Schmidt, S.K. (2012) 'Who cares about nationality? The path-dependent case law of the ECJ from goods to citizens', *Journal of European Public Policy* 19(1): 8–24.
Sindbjerg Martinsen, D. and Vrangbaek, K. (2008) 'The Europeanization of health care governance – implementing the market imperatives of Europe', *Public Administration* 86(1): 169–84.
Somek, A. (2008a) 'Das europäische Sozialmodell: Diskriminierungsschutz und Wettbewerb', *Juridikum* 2008(3): 118–25.
Somek, A. (2008b) *Individualism: An Essay on the Authority of the European Union*, Oxford: Oxford University Press.
Stone Sweet, A. (2004) *The Judicial Construction of Europe*, Oxford: Oxford University Press.
Stone Sweet, A. and Stranz, K. (2012) 'Rights adjudication and constitutional pluralism in Germany and Europe', *Journal of European Public Policy* 19(1): 92–108.
Vauchez, A. (2007) 'Embedded law. Political sociology of the European Community of law: elements of a renewed research agenda', *EUI Working Papers RSCAS 2007/23*, Florence: Robert Schuman Centre for Advanced Studies.
Weiler, J.H.H. and Lockhart, N.J.S. (1995) '"Taking rights seriously" seriously: the European Court of Justice and its fundamental rights jurisprudence', *Common Market Law Review* 32(1): 51–94.
Wind, M., Sindbjerg Martinsen, D. and Pons Rotger, G. (2009) 'The uneven legal push for Europe: questioning variation when national courts go to Europe', *European Union Politics* 10(1): 63–88.
Wollenschläger, F. (2011) 'A new fundamental freedom beyond market integration: Union citizenship and its dynamics for shifting the economic paradigm of European integration', *European Law Journal* 17(1): 1–34.

Index